berlin

shop

eat

sleep

berlin shop · eat · sleep

isbn 90 5767 087 9

daniel   monika

author daniel haaksman

final editing zahra sethna

photography monika rehberger

graphic design oranje vormgevers, eindhoven

project guidance joyce enthoven & sasja lagendijk, mo' media

printing office deckers druk, beveren (b)

preface

Berlin bubbles. The past year has witnessed the opening of a bevy
of new shops and restaurants. Berlin's rich history contributes to an
amazing mix of trend-setting fashion boutiques, austere interiors and
hip clubs & cocktail lounges. And with many different varieties of
cuisine, gorgeous restaurants and talented chefs, Berlin is making
a name for itself in the culinary field.

This guide directs you through the side streets of Kurfürstendamm
to the hottest spots in Berlin. We will once again lead you to 200
addresses we've found essential enough to highlight in this guide.
These span mom-and-pop stores run by dedicated shopkeepers to
grand specialty boutiques. Included are restaurants serving-up both
hearty meals and unique ambiances suited to please any taste. And
not to be omitted are hotels where you can relish a pleasant stay in
one of their incomparable rooms. To make your visit to Berlin complete,
we've also provided some additional suggestions in the back of the book.

A few addresses listed in the previous edition are no longer valid and
have been replaced. Chances are you will discover new "hotspots"
that aren't mentioned in this guide. If you find fault with an entry or
feel as if there's something we've overlooked, or if you have a general
comment, please let us know! Our address is listed in the back of this
book.

Enjoy Berlin!

shop   **eat**   **sleep**

iconography

All addresses are marked with one or more icons. These will help you to discern whether an establishment is for shopping, eating & drinking, and/or sleeping. In the back of the guide, you'll find a complete map of Berlin. Every neighborhood is delineated in segments on this map. The number of each segment refers to its page number in the guide. The color of the number refers to the icons listed in the map's legend and subsequently to the address's distinction as a place for shopping, eating or sleeping.

tear-away bookmark

You can make a bookmark from the backside of the plastic cover.
Pull off the book's cover and tear away the strip with the symbols,
on the perforated line. This strip can now be easily used as a
bookmark by snapping the side of marker into the spiral rings.

payment and price indication

For payment with credit cards, we've only complied information on
MasterCard, Visa and American Express. In some establishments,
presumably, other cards are accepted as forms of payment as well.
The price indicated for restaurants is the average price per main
course, unless otherwise noted. Prices indicated for hotels and
B&Bs are based on minimum rates for a double room for one night.

independent editing

To clarify, we do not accept payment in exchange for listing or
endorsing any place or business highlighted in this guide, neither
for texts nor photos. All texts are selected and written by our
independent editorial team.

contents

Prenzlauer Berg

This working class neighborhood in the former East Berlin has experienced a major transformation lately. This guide focuses on the central part of the area, framed by Prenzlauer Allee to the east, Kastanienallee to the west, and Stargaderstrasse to the north. Be sure to explore the beautiful squares of Kollwitzplatz, Wasserturmplatz and Helmholtzplatz – where the real life of the city takes place. Trendy Kastanienallee is the place to find many restaurants and bars. Check out magazines like 'Flyer' or 'Zitty' to find out events taking place on weekends. If you're up for something for mellow, Prenzlauer Berg is a beautiful area to stroll – day or night.

Prenzlauer Berg

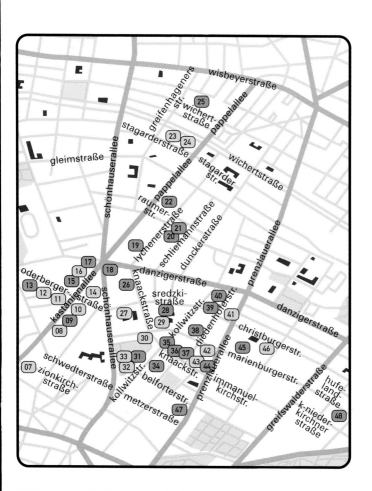

PEGS
art, design, living

KASTANIENALLEE 55 **TELEPHONE** 44 04 32 75 WWW.PEGSBERLIN.COM
OPENING HOURS MON-FRI 12.00-20.00, SAT 10.00-16.00
CREDIT CARDS NONE **U-BAHNHOF** ROSENTHALERPLATZ

07

Kastanienallee is one of the best streets for shopping in this part of the city, and PEGS is a great place to start. You'll come to it quickly if you walk up from Mitte. Full of 'accessories for living,' as the store itself defines it, you'll find glasses, lamps, vases, ceramics and small furniture. Everything is bright and lively, and some of the ceramics can be decorated exactly the way you want them.

Mont Klamott

outdoor wear

KASTANIENALLEE 83 **TELEPHONE** 44 82 590
OPENING HOURS MON-FRI 10.00-20.00, SAT 10.00-16.00
CREDIT CARDS NONE **U-BAHNHOF** EBERSWALDERSTRASSE

Berlin may not be surrounded by mountains, but its winters are cold enough to require just the right equipment. Mont Klamott is the place to find all the clothing to keep you well protected from wind, rain and snow. They stock outerwear, boots, sleeping bags, tents and gear for mountaineers, hikers and outdoorsmen of all kinds. This kind of apparel has become fashionable in an urban setting as well; so don't be surprised to see the occasional Hip Hop fan amongst the mountaineers preparing for their next expedition.

Viennese coffee house culture is the inspiration at Sowohlalsauch, where a massive Gustav Klimt graces the wall and the odd waltz can still be heard. Mostly, however, expect to hear typical Berlin coffee house music such as Air, Thievery Corporation or Kruder & Dorfmeister. The food here is equally eclectic - Austrian with a continental spin. The huge and diverse menu is excellent, but for a real taste of Austria, venture into Kreuzberg.

Sowohlalsauch

viennese coffee house

KOLLWITZSTRASSE 88 **TELEPHONE** 33 29 311
OPENING HOURS DAILY FROM 09.00-02.00
CREDIT CARDS NONE **PRICE** € 6 **U-BAHNHOF** SENEFELDERPLATZ

This store brings to mind the cover of the phenomenal Beatles album for which it is named. You're more likely to find trendy clothes from the 70s and early 80s than from the mod era at this second hand store, but with a good eye and a little luck you can sometimes score a winner. Every once in a while it's even possible to dig up a men's suit from the 1940s. But whatever you find, it's sure to be good, and the prices are great too!

Sgt. Peppers
selected second hand

KASTANIENALLEE 91/92 **TELEPHONE** 44 81 121
OPENING HOURS MON–FRI 12.00-19.00, SAT 11.00-16.00
CREDIT CARDS MASTERCARD, VISA **U-BAHNHOF** EBERSWALDERSTRASSE

Thatchers
for party girls and boys

ALTE SCHÖNHAUSERSTRASSE 7 **TELEPHONE** 24 62 77 51
OPENING HOURS MON-FRI 12.00-19.00, SAT 12.00-16.00 **CREDIT CARDS** NONE
U-BAHNHOF ROSA-LUXEMBURG-PLATZ OR WEINMEISTERSTRASSE

No, this store doesn't have anything to do with conservative British Prime Ministers. It's the flagship store of two young Berlin designers who concoct extravagant and eye-catching clothes. If you are a party girl (or boy) who likes to look good and show off in clubs and at gatherings, this is the place for you. You'll will always find what's hot, making you the hottest thing in town.

Pauls Boutique

check your head

ODERBERGERSTRASSE 47 **TELEPHONE** 44 03 37 37
OPENING HOURS MON–FRI 12.00-20.00, SAT 12.00-18.00
CREDIT CARDS NONE **U-BAHNHOF** EBERSWALDERSTRASSE

This store gets its name from the Beastie Boys' second album, which was dedicated to an imaginary boutique in Brooklyn. In fact, this store looks almost exactly like the one on the cover of the album. It's full of 1970s-style sneakers, cool T-shirts, sports bags, retro tracksuits, military clothing, funk and nu jazz records and weird sunglasses. Despite its 'boyish' feel, Beastie girls will be pleased here too. The store's hours are written with a 'circa', so make sure you call before dropping by.

Here the raw fish, sticky rice and seaweed delicacies you love so much are served on small wooden ships - too beautiful to be eaten quickly. So take some time to chat with your neighbor. The seating around the square-shaped bar is perfect for small talk. If you aren't in the mood to chat, it's also fun to watch the Japanese chef in the center of the bar, as he slices and rolls his fine fish creations. Don't forget to try the Miso soup for € 3; it's fantastic.

Sushi Bar Ky

japan's greatest hits

ODERBERGERSTRASSE 40 **TELEPHONE** 44 05 89 69
OPENING HOURS DAILY 17.00-23.30
CREDIT CARDS NONE **PRICE** MENU € 7 **U-BAHNHOF** EBERSWALDERSTRASSE

13

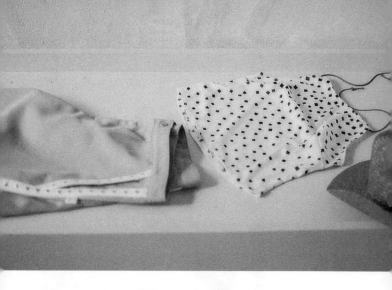

Betty Bund

elaborate street fashion

ODERBERGERSTRASSE 6 **TELEPHONE** 21 72 038
OPENING HOURS MON–FRI 12.00-20.00, SAT 11.00-16.00
CREDIT CARDS VISA, MASTERCARD **U-BAHNHOF** EBERSWALDERSTRASSE

These days, casual and comfortable clothes are everywhere. So how does a fashion-conscious person stay comfortable and still look sharp? By shopping at Betty Bund, that's how! This Berlin-based designer puts an emphasis on function and calls her clothing line 'Body tools for OK people.' We say these garments are better than OK; zips, small bags and light-yet-durable fabrics make them extra special. Betty Bund's clothes are perfect for any occasion - from a fancy dinner at Gendarmenmarkt to a night in an illegal basement club. Whatever you choose, you'll be dressed to kill.

Come drink your troubles away at this relic of a bar.
Through the clouds of cigarette smoke you'll just be able
to make out the crowds of students and creative types -
the kind of people who keep this place busy day and
night. Perhaps they love it for the cheap drinks... vodka
on ice is only € 2.

Schwarz-Sauer
classic bar

KASTANIENALLEE 13 **TELEPHONE** 44 85 633
OPENING HOURS DAILY 08.00-05.00
CREDIT CARDS NONE **U-BAHNHOF** EBERSWALDERSTRASSE

Eisdieler

homegrown street and sportswear

KASTANIENALLEE 12 **TELEPHONE** 28 57 351 WWW.EISDIELER.DE
OPENING HOURS MON-FRI 12.00-20.00, SAT 12.00-18.00
CREDIT CARDS VISA, MASTERCARD **U-BAHNHOF** EBERSWALDERSTRASSE

This store is a true Berlin original. You might see the name all over town,
but don't ask what it means. There's really no translation for it in English.
The story is as follows: originally located in a former gelateria, the
store's owners came up with the name by playing with the pronuncia-
tion and meanings of the words 'ice', 'dealer' and 'diele' - the German
word for wooden tiles. Although the name doesn't make sense, it
became an instant hit and a new label was born. It has now been
printed on sportswear, board gear and recycled army t-shirts and is
sold exclusively in this store.

Although Germany is famous for them, it's hard to find a proper 'biergarten' in Berlin. These open-air garden-restaurants are great for sitting outside having food and drinking beer. Prater is one of the few in the city and undoubtedly one of the most beautiful. The restaurant's garden is crammed in summer with Berliners enjoying their beer and the meaty Bavarian and Austrian menu. Students and journalists, locals and actors all come to Prater. Sausages sizzle on the grill, but there are also salads and vegetarian plates. Try the 'Rindsgeschnetzeltes', sliced beefsteak in a creamy pepper sauce for € 12, which is great. In the winter, enjoy a good meal indoors or show up on a Sunday afternoon, when you can even enjoy some traditional dancing.

Prater
beer garden

KASTANIENALLEE 7-9 **TELEPHONE** 44 85 688
OPENING HOURS MON-FRI 18.00-01.00, SAT, SUN FROM 14.00
CREDIT CARDS NONE **PRICE** € 10 **U-BAHNHOF** EBERSWALDERSTRASSE

17

One of Berlin's most famous culinary specialties is 'currywurst' - a pork sausage spiced with curry and ketchup. There has long been a debate about who cooks the best currywurst in town, and in the former East Berlin the winner surely has to be Konnopke's Imbiß on Schönhauser Allee. This restaurant was founded in 1930 and ever since has been a magnet for 'wurst' lovers. They serve six variations of currywurst as well as salads and, of course, beer. Experts say it's the intestine wrapped around the pork meat that makes Konnopke's currywurst delicious. Others believe it's the homemade ketchup. It's probably best to come and decide for yourself.

Konnopke's Imbiß
original berliner wurst

SCHÖNHAUSER ALLEE 44A **TELEPHONE** 44 27 765
OPENING HOURS MON–FRI 06.30-20.00
CREDIT CARDS NONE **PRICE** SNACK € 1.50 **U-BAHNHOF** EBERSWALDERSTRASSE

Tamra
middle eastern and arabic specialities

LYCHENERSTRASSE 13 **TELEPHONE** 47 37 49 61
OPENING HOURS SUN-THU 11.00-01.00, FRI-SAT 11.00-02.00 **CREDIT CARDS** NONE
PRICE € 4 **U-BAHNHOF** EBERSWALDERSTRASSE

While most Middle Eastern and Arabic restaurants in Berlin are run by Lebanese, Egyptians or Moroccans, Tamra is run by Iraqis. You might be able to spot the differences on the menu. Some dishes, like biriyani, are of Indian origin but are common in Iraqi cuisine. There is also the usual range of Middle Eastern dishes, from shoarma to falafel, delicious couscous salad, fish dishes and vegetable salads. This is one of the best options for this cuisine in Prenzlauer Berg.

Drei

california dreaming

LYCHENERSTRASSE 30 **TELEPHONE** 44 73 84 71
OPENING HOURS DAILY 10.00-02.00
CREDIT CARDS NONE **PRICE** € 10 **S-BAHNHOF** EBERSWALDERSTRASSE

Drei opened recently and quickly became an in-place for Prenzlauer Berg's media types and 'digerati'. Inside is a bar, lounge and restaurant. Start your evening at the bar with a nice aperitif or cocktail, then make your way to the restaurant for Californian or Asian inspired dishes. Later, relax in the lounge with a fat cigar and another cocktail. If you come early, you can enjoy Drei's happy hour, which is from 18.00 to 20.00.

This snack bar is so small it would be easy to pass it by, if not for the big sign on the door reading 'TOAST'. Come in for freshly made sandwiches, toasts and panini, plus a huge range of hot and cold drinks. Your UFO-shaped sandwich, made with delicious bread and stuffed with fresh ingredients such as mozzarella and tomato, is so much fun to look at you might not want to eat it. But remember what your mother said, and please don't play with your food!

Toast
snack bar

RAUMERSTRASSE 12 **TELEPHONE** 44 05 61 89
OPENING HOURS MON-FRI 08.00-22.00, SAT 09.00-22.00, SUN 10.00-22.00
CREDIT CARDS NONE **PRICE** SANDWICH € 3 **U-BAHNHOF** EBERSWALDERSTRASSE

Inspired by a visit to the house of Mexican painter Frida Kahlo, this restaurant's owner painted it shades of brown and green. You almost feel like you're sitting in one of Kahlo's famous paintings as you feast on Mexican food. Prices are moderate, and at night the restaurant becomes one of the most popular bars in the area. More than 80 different cocktails are available, plus various international wines. The cook is Mexican, you can be sure that the food, as well as the temperament, is authentic.

Frida Kahlo
mexican food

LYCHENERSTRASSE 37 **TELEPHONE** 44 57 016
OPENING HOURS DAILY 10.00-02.00
CREDIT CARDS NONE **PRICE** € 7 **U-BAHNHOF** EBERSWALDERSTRASSE

Headhunters
no appointment needed

STARGARDERSTRASSE CORNER GETHSEMANSTRASSE **TELEPHONE** 44 73 69 96
OPENING HOURS TUE-FRI 11.00-19.00, SAT 11-16.00
CREDIT CARDS NONE **U-BAHNHOF** EBERSWALDERSTRASSE

When the need for a hair cut hits, head for Headhunters. No appointment is needed here, although you will need a little patience. Draw a number, sit down and wait your turn. When the time comes, have a seat and for just € 10 the hairdressers at Headhunters will get you all cleaned up. It's not the best place for a perm or anything too complicated, but they work quickly so if you need just a trim, it's perfect. Sometimes it's so busy it can take up to an hour to get seated, but everyone here likes to chat, so you might be able to catch up on the latest gossip.

Antikhandlung

fine antiques

STARGARDERSTRASSE 75 **TELEPHONE** 44 73 63 96
OPENING HOURS MON–FRI 13.30-18.30, SAT 10.00-14.00 AND BY APPOINTMENT
CREDIT CARDS NONE **U-BAHNHOF** EBERSWALDERSTRASSE

You can tell by the aroma of this store that it sells antiques. Antikhandlung smells of fresh flowers and old furniture. Stocked full of German antiques from the late 19th century, plus some Art Nouveau and early 20th century pieces, each item is reasonably priced, so there's no haggling here. The ideal shop for new collectors, the range of products here is excellent: from pieces as small as lamps to as large as wardrobes, you'll find everything for a tasteful home.

Berlin has a huge Russian community, and there are two-dozen restaurants catering to that cuisine. Voland is considered one of the best. Luckily, the food is not exclusively based on meat. Try for example the vegetarian Borschtsch soup. The ravioli-like Pelmenis are handmade and taste fantastic. If you fancy a drink, flip through the five-page list and chose between eight different types of vodka, wine from the Krim or Schnaps from Armenia. An average meal is just € 10, so for an eating adventure it's definitely worth a try. If you are lucky, you'll be able to dine during a reading by a Russian author.

Voland
borscht and vodka

WICHERTSTRASSE 63 **TELEPHONE** 44 40 422
OPENING HOURS DAILY 18.00-02.00
CREDIT CARDS NONE **PRICE** € 10 **U-BAHNHOF** SCHNHAUSERALLEE

The restored Kulturbrauerei is a huge space with cinemas, concert halls, restaurants and clubs. One of these is Soda, a restaurant/lounge/club where jazz is played and authors recite their works. (The owners are trying to revive the atmosphere of 1920s Berlin). The restaurant serves light, international dishes. After dinner, move to the upstairs club where house, soul and salsa music are played to a young and trendy crowd. For all-around entertainment, Soda is the best place to get a start on an evening in Prenzlauer Berg.

Soda
lounging, eating and clubbing

KNACKSTRASSE 60 **TELEPHONE** 44 05 87 08 WWW.SODA-CLUB-BERLIN.DE
OPENING HOURS TUE-SUN 20.00-03.00, FRI, SAT 20.00-05.00
CREDIT CARDS NONE **PRICE** € 10 **U-BAHNHOF** EBERSWALDERSTRASSE

Furniture
fantastic plastic

SREDZKISTRASSE 22 **TELEPHONE** 44 34 21 57
OPENING HOURS TUE 12.30-19.00, WED 14.00-19.00, THU 12.30-20.00, FRI 12.30-19.00,
SAT 12.30-16.00 **CREDIT CARDS** NONE **U-BAHNHOF** EBERSWALDERSTRASSE

If you are a real antique buff then you probably enjoy rummaging around flea markets, and don't mind the early mornings and occasionally fruitless journeys. But if you're the type of person who would rather take it easy, stay in bed and shop later in the day, then you'll definitely want to check out Furniture, on Sredzkistrasse. Kerstin Jürgens has a passion for collecting furniture and interior design from the 1960s and 70s. Her store carries everything from psychedelic tapestries to plastic lamps, chairs, drawers, sofas, beads, old Playboy magazines and kitchen stuff. Most of it is plastic, and its all pretty fantastic.

Ostwind

chinese bistro and restaurant

HUSEMANNSTRASSE 13 **TELEPHONE** 44 15 951
OPENING HOURS MON-FRI 11.00-13.00 & 18.00-01.00, SAT, SUN 10.00-01.00
CREDIT CARDS NONE **PRICE** € 9 **U-BAHNHOF** EBERSWALDERSTRASSE

Ostwind is serious about its food. You won't find any Chinese kitsch here, just authentic and original Chinese cooking. When visiting at lunchtime, try the spring rolls, won-ton soup, salads or rice dishes served fast food style at modest prices. In the evening, Ostwind becomes a proper restaurant, with a cozy atmosphere and friendly service. Try the delicious jasmine duck, which is only € 12.

Not surprisingly, this store sells Moroccan furniture and interiors. Inside, it feels like an oriental market (minus the food and cattle). As music blasts, the owner sits in a corner with friends, chatting and laughing over a strong cup of tea. The store is full of Moroccan and Asian furniture, pottery, jewelry, lamps, carpets, brass and metallic lanterns, small boxes made of wood from the thuja-root and dozens of other things that you associate with the orient. If the owner has time for a quick chat, he may even serve you tea.

Marrakesch
all oriental

HUSEMANNSTRASSE 9 **TELEPHONE** 44 35 63 86
OPENING HOURS MON–FRI 12.00-20.00
CREDIT CARDS VISA, MASTERCARD **PRICE** € 8 **U-BAHNHOF** EBERSWALDERSTRASSE

Sure, you've heard of antique furniture, but what about antique fashion? Check out 'Falbala', where the fashion is more than 70 years old. In fact, the oldest garment is from 1900, and the youngest is from the mid 1970s. Everything here is authentic and comes from private collectors; so don't worry about finding new pieces that are made to look old. Most of the shoes, hats, bags, furs, skirts, shirts and gowns are for women, but there is also some men's clothing. If you're into fashion and history, you'll love this store.

Falbala
antique fashion

 KNAACKSTRASSE 43 **TELEPHONE** 44 05 10 82
OPENING HOURS MON-FRI 13.00-18.00, SAT 12.00-14.00
CREDIT CARDS VISA, MASTERCARD, AMEX **U-BAHNHOF** SENEFELDERPLATZ

30

Vannini
homemade italian ice cream

KOLLWITZSTRASSE 59 **TELEPHONE** 44 05 55 08
OPENING HOURS DAILY 12.00-24.00
CREDIT CARDS NONE **U-BAHNHOF** SENEFELDERPLATZ

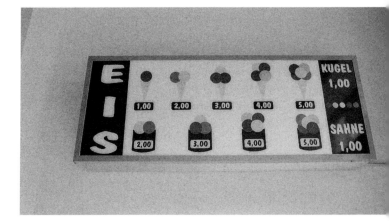

Prenzlauer Berg only has a few Italian 'gelaterias'. Vannini is one of them, and the ice here tastes so good, people come from all over the city just to enjoy the fresh and fruity ice creams. Try Smurf ice cream, which tastes like bubble gum, or the carrot-orange ice cream, which is a pretty unique combination. It's so delicious you'll immediately wonder how they manage to make it taste so good, especially since no artificial flavors are added.

Monticello

all flowered out

KOLLWITZSTRASSE 45 **TELEPHONE** 44 05 90 90
OPENING HOURS MON-FRI 09.00-20.00, SAT 09.00-16.00, SUN 12.00-16.00
CREDIT CARDS VISA, MASTERCARD **U-BAHNHOF** SENEFELDERPLATZ

Flower lovers don't miss a trip to Monticello, which calls itself a 'Floristeria'. There's a definite air of the Mediterranean here as you walk through big wreaths of colorful flowers, and browse the terracotta pots full of a wide range of plants and fresh flowers. Whether you need roses for a romantic rendezvous, tulips for your grandmother or small plants for your balcony, you'll find it here. Downstairs are books about gardening and plants, plus a range of beautiful wrapping paper. With classical music and friendly service, there might not be a better place for to 'say it with flowers'.

Kollwitz 45

tres chic

KOLLWITZSTRASSE 45 **TELEPHONE** 44 01 04 13 WWW.KOLLWITZ45.DE
OPENING HOURS MON–FRI 11.00-20.00, SAT 11.00-16.00
CREDIT CARDS VISA, MASTERCARD **U-BAHNHOF** SENEFELDERPLATZ

Whether you live in an urban apartment with high
ceilings and wooden floors or in a house in the country,
Katja Wilhelm and partner Stephan Dass, have some
great ideas for decorating your living space. They are the
interior design consultants who run Kollwitz 45, a store
that Wilhelm says stocks, "functional furniture with a
touch of sensuality and poetry." From A(lias) to Z(anotta),
everything at Kollwitz 45 has a special edge. This store
carries every great design from every imaginable place!

If you've never been to Spain, you can at least get a taste of the country at Aragon Tapas bar. The restaurant offers a sampling of the tastes of the Iberian Peninsula with delicacies from all over the country. No main dishes are served here, just scrumptious snacks like bocadillos, small meat-plates, salads, baked vegetables, cheese and a good list of Spanish wines, all at modest prices. The owner has made the establishment so authentic that its even possible to pay in Pesetas! On Monday evenings, wine, beer and tequila are only 100 PTAs per glass. Be there early, as the cozy basement bar only has a few seats.

Aragon Tapas Bar

spanish snacks

DIEDENHOFERSTRASSE 6 **TELEPHONE** 44 06 319
OPENING HOURS DAILY 19.00-03.00
CREDIT CARDS NONE **PRICE** MENU € 8 **U-BAHNHOF** SENEFELDERPLATZ

Anita Wronski
hanging around

KNAACKSTRASSE 26-28 **TELEPHONE** 44 28 483
OPENING HOURS MON–FRI 09.00-02.00, SAT, SUN 10.00-02.00
CREDIT CARDS NONE **PRICE** € 5 **U-BAHNHOF** SENEFELDERPLATZ

The Knaackstrasse, which is located at the Wasserturmplatz, hosts
a variety of bars and cafés... but the Anita Wronski is surely the one
where you can catch the most afternoon sun while lazing around on
the terrace with a coffee or a small snack. Who are all these people
spending their time hanging around, you might wonder... Are they
students, literati, actors or musicians? No one seems to know. Although
this type of people seems to be a dying species in other European
capitals, in Berlin they still thrive, and in Prenzlauer Berg the Anita
Wronski is their temple.

Kost.Bar

'alpian' delights

KNAACKSTRASSE 24 **TELEPHONE** 43 73 55 74
OPENING HOURS MON-FRI 14.00-02.00, SAT, SUN 10.00-02.00
CREDIT CARDS VISA **PRICE** € 8 **U-BAHNHOF** SENEFELDERPLATZ

In spite of increasing tourism in the Wasserturmplatz area, the Kost.Bar is a precious gem that manages to remain tourist free. From the outside, this small restaurant doesn't look very special, but the food served here is absolutely outstanding. It is Alpian-style cuisine, meaning food from the area surrounding Bohemia, Austria and Northern Italy. Pasta is a regular ingredient on the weekly menu, and so is venison (deer). Try some fantastic 'Serviettenknödel' for € 8, with a bottle of Paul Blanck wine for just € 13. You'll be thrilled with the food's freshness and amazed at the unbelievably low prices for such high quality cooking.

You've just finished a delicious dinner at one of the restaurants on Kollwitzplatz or Wasserturmplatz, and now you need a 'digestiv' or a long drink. Well stretch your legs and have a seat at the Hausbar, where you'll get cocktails and mixed drinks for € 5 to € 10. The place draws an eclectic crowd and features a mixed soundtrack of Cuban music, Downtempo and Rock. If you're interested in meeting Berliners, this is a good place to do it, as people like to rub shoulders here.

Hausbar
cozy drinking

RYKESTRASSE 54 **TELEPHONE** 44 04 76 06
OPENING HOURS DAILY 19.00-05.00
CREDIT CARDS NONE **U-BAHNHOF** SENEFELDERPLATZ

It's quite difficult to find a good, original Thai restaurant in Europe. You can usually tell by one glance at the menu; if duck soup is offered as an appetizer, you know you've found the real deal. Mao Thai is as authentic as you can get. Try the chicken stew or the roasted duck in oyster sauce for € 13. You'll feel like you are sitting in a secret Bangkok café, off the beaten track. Dinner at Mao Thai's will make you want to pack your bags and head for Thailand. It will certainly give you a taste of things to come.

Mao Thai

authentic thai food

38

WÖRTHERSTRASSE 30 **TELEPHONE** 44 19 261
OPENING HOURS SUN–THU 12.00-00.00, FRI, SAT 12.00-01.00
CREDIT CARDS AMEX, VISA, MASTERCARD **PRICE** € 7 **U-BAHNHOF** SENEFELDERPLATZ

Kamun

cheap and simple

KASTANIENALLEE 87 **TELEPHONE** NO
OPENING HOURS DAILY 12.00-24.00
CREDIT CARDS NONE **PRICE** € 3 **U-BAHNHOF** EBERSWALDERSTRASSE

Kamun is a great place for Middle Eastern food. The prices are so low that it's even easy to overlook the somewhat dry whole wheat pita bread. Try the roasted turkey liver for € 2.50 or have a plate of beans for € 3. Strong black tea and Indian bread, naan, are free.

WKG
meat free zone

KOLLWITZSTRASSE 90 **TELEPHONE** 44 05 64 44
OPENING HOURS SUN-FRI 12.00-22.00
CREDIT CARDS NONE **PRICE** € 4 **U-BAHNHOF** EBERSWALDERSTRASSE

As you walk through Berlin, you might notice the local penchant for abbreviations. There are clubs called WMF or NBI, galleries called FFWD and NBK, and then there is WKG. This stands for 'Wir kochen Gemüse,' which means this place only cooks vegetarian food. The menu is rich, with everything a good vegetarian café and take-away can offer. Try the veggie burgers, tofu ravioli, green cakes or salads and if you're thirsty have some freshly squeezed apple, carrot or orange juice. With great service and outdoor seating in the summer, this truly is veggie heaven!

The man behind the sales counter can be a little grumpy, but otherwise Freak Out is an excellent record store, stocking tons of vinyl and CDs. The selection crosses all important underground music genres: from Techno to Trip Hop, from Indie-Rock to 60s Soul and Garage-Punk. Freak Out has everything a dedicated music lover yearns for, and the second-hand section has an equally impressive and broad range of musical styles. If you have time to wait in line, you can listen to the records and CDs before buying them.

Freak Out
from indie rock to 60s soul

RYKESTRASSE 23 **TELEPHONE** 44 27 615
OPENING HOURS MON-SAT 11.30-19.30
CREDIT CARDS VISA **U-BAHNHOF** EBERSWALDERSTRASSE

Even the biggest wine aficionados might need help choosing from the selection of more than 700 wines at Baumgart & Braun. A delicate white wine to go with pasta? A fruity Chardonnay to complement a meat dish? Maybe a nice bottle of champagne, as a present for a friend? Marcus Baumgart will lead you to the perfect choice. He knows his stock like the back of his hand, and will gladly answer your questions and share his expertise. Even if your wallet is not stuffed, Baumgart will make sure you leave his store happy.

Baumgart & Braun
wine, wine, wine

WÖRTHERSTRASSE 30 **TELEPHONE** 44 10 235
OPENING HOURS MON-FRI 12.00-20.00, SAT 10.00-15.00
CREDIT CARDS VISA **U-BAHNHOF** SENEFELDERPLATZ

Schelpmeier
women's fashion

RYKESTRASSE 1 CORNER KNACKSTRASSE **TELEPHONE** 39 26 781
OPENING HOURS MON-FRI 11.00-19.00, SAT 11.00-16.00
CREDIT CARDS VISA, MASTERCARD **U-BAHNHOF** EBERSWALDERSTRASSE

Fashion can sometimes be a little intimidating. That's why Schelpmeier is such a pleasant place to look around. You'll feel welcome here, even if you don't have much money and just want to look around at what's in stock. The store's owner makes some of the clothes here, while the rest come from young, independent designers from Scandinavia, Holland and Germany. These are chic and practical clothes that can be combined with every wardrobe basic. Everything has a classic cut and is made from colorful, natural fabrics. You'll quickly find these becoming your new favorite clothes.

Suriya Kanthi

fine sri lankan food

KNAACKSTRASSE 4 **TELEPHONE** 44 25 101
OPENING HOURS DAILY 12.00-01.00
CREDIT CARDS NONE **PRICE** € 7 **U-BAHNHOF** SENEFELDERPLATZ

Suriya Kanthi is one of the few Sri Lankan restaurants in all of Germany, and it's definitely the only one that buys its ingredients from eco-groceries and butchers. Consequently, the food is all totally fresh and, since most of the dishes contain coconut milk, gentle on your stomach. The special mix of roasted and ground spices makes an excellent impression, and the friendly service and bright, well-conceived interior does the rest. Even the prices are good! When a delegation of Sri Lankan ministers is in town, they always visit Suriya Kanthi. What could be a better compliment?

In the area of Italy known as Ligury, 'cenone' means a big meal. People sit at long tables where they are treated to a 17-course eating extravaganza. Twice a month, on Wednesdays, Cenone the restaurant provides a similar feast (this time with only seven courses) for € 35. Be sure to make a reservation, as these gorge-fests are extremely popular amongst Berlin's 'Tuscany population', as Italy-loving Germans are called. In addition to the marathon meal, Cenone offers take out food, including a huge range of olive oils, wine, antipasti, bacon, cheeses and salsas. If you are still hungry after your big meal, you can take something to go. Course number 8, perhaps.

Cenone
big italian meals

MARIENBURGERSTRASSE 48 **TELEPHONE** 44 01 77 35
OPENING HOURS DAILY 10.00-24.00
CREDIT CARDS NONE **PRICE** € 9 **U-BAHNHOF** SENEFELDERPLATZ 45

If you like furniture and accessories from around the globe, check out Gecko. There is a great range of small decorative pieces, jewelry, furniture and clothes from dozens of countries. Try on a beautiful sari or a Japanese kimono. Have a seat in a Moroccan chair or take a look at the oriental gardening lamps hanging from the ceiling. You can travel the world right in this store, and create a beautiful ambience for your home that proves how open-minded and individualistic you really are.

Gecko
global interiors

WINSSTRASSE 51 **TELEPHONE** 44 39 034
OPENING HOURS MON-FRI 11.00-19.30, SAT 11.00-15.00
CREDIT CARDS VISA, MASTERCARD **U-BAHNHOF** EBERSWALDERSTRASSE

Luxusbar
drink, drank, drunk

BELFORTERSTRASSE 18 **TELEPHONE** 44 34 15 14
OPENING HOURS DAILY 19.00-05.00
CREDIT CARDS NONE **U-BAHNHOF** SENEFELDERPLATZ

47

Don't expect luxury from Luxusbar...the name if pure irony. Located
in a former butchery, the interior is very basic. However, cocktails and
drinks are cheap and conversation is free. In winter, the atmosphere
inside is so smoky you get an instant nicotine rush when you walk in
the room. The minuscule bar is very popular with Prenzlauer Berg's
creative types, and other people who like to drink a lot.

Chez Maurice

le savoir vivre

BÖTZOWSTRASSE 39 **TELEPHONE** 42 80 47 23
OPENING HOURS DAILY 18.30-24.00
CREDIT CARDS NONE **PRICE** € 14 **TRAM** 2, 3, 4

48

A little off the beaten track from Prenzlauer Berg's main drag, Chez Maurice is the kind of restaurant that you'll immediately fall in love with. Thankfully, the restaurant does without the ironed napkins and arrogant waiters. The atmosphere here is very relaxed and the staff is very friendly and always in for a laugh. Last but not least, the food is superb. Try the delicious carpaccio for starters, and then move on to duck breast with pepper cream sauce. Complement your meal with an excellent and affordable wine, and you'll be truly spoiled. At around € 25, you'll be hard pressed to get a better French meal in more comfortable surroundings anywhere. Don't miss it.

Mitte

Mitte, the part of Berlin where the government and administration offices are, is also home to the Reichstag and the Brandenburg gate. Some of Berlin's biggest theatres, opera houses and museums, and its most exclusive shops and hotels, are located here. Last but not least, this is the area where young Berliners do their shopping and partying. North of Unter den Linden, in the Scheunenviertel quarter, the city's cultural scene flourishes, with bars, restaurants, nightclubs, theatres, galleries and cinemas. The restored area south of Unter den Linden and alongside Friedrichstrasse is where the elite shop and stay. To avoid the tourist traps, follow our guide as we steer you off Hackesche Höfe and through the streets north of Oranienburgerstrasse and east of Rosenthaler-strasse. You'll find quiet, romantic bars and restaurants and lots of small and interesting shops.

Mitte

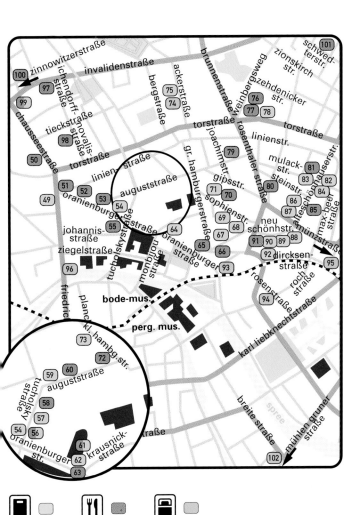

Musikmarkt
musically minded

FRIEDRICHSTRASSE 129 **TELEPHONE** 28 59 144
OPENING HOURS MON-FRI 10.00-20.00, SAT 10.00-16.00
CREDIT CARDS NONE **U-BAHNHOF** ORANIENBURGER TOR

Vinyl junkies beware: this store may become your newest addiction.
Don't even think of spending less than two hours here. A true goldmine,
Musikmarkt has tons of records and CDs of all varieties. The top floor
has a good selection of new releases in Indie-Rock, Hip Hop, House
and Reggae, but the basement is where it's really happening. There's
a huge selection of second-hand music, from Funk to Rap, to Gothic Rock
and East German or Polish Jazz rarities. Best of all are the prices, which
are fantastically low, as well as the helpful and knowledgeable staff.

Although the name might be a bit misleading, this place is both a restaurant and bar. Its small, basic interior belies the fact that it is one of Mitte's best and most reasonably priced Spanish restaurants. The generous fish plate entrée is € 16; half a liter of excellent Spanish wine € 12; and if you throw in a small tapas plate, you can have a delicious and filling meal without breaking the bank! The lamb dishes are also superb. Make sure you make a reservation early, as it can fill up quickly.

Bar-Celona

olé

HANNOVERSCHESTRASSE 2 **TELEPHONE** 28 29 156
OPENING HOURS SUN–WED 12.00-01.00, THU–SAT 12.00-02.00
CREDIT CARDS VISA **PRICE** € 8 **U-BAHNHOF** ORANIENBURGER TOR

Dada, the international nihilist, anarchist art movement, had a very strong following amongst Berlin artists of the early 1910s. Even today, it has its dedicated followers, and Azzeaz Salah is one of them. An actor and theater director, Salah finances his theatrical projects by running the Dada Falafel snack bar. Dada has the best pan-Arabian cuisine in Mitte, offering falafel, shoarma and various salads, all made with superfresh ingredients. Salah will take good care of you, and you might even get to rub shoulders with some of the actors he's currently working with; they all go to Dada Falafel after rehearsals.

Dada Falafel
pan-arabian food

LINIENSTRASSE 132 **TELEPHONE** 28 28 317
OPENING HOURS DAILY 11.00-02.00
CREDIT CARDS NONE **PRICE** € 5 **U-BAHNHOF** ORANIENBURGER TOR

Beckers Fritten
delicious french fries

ORANIENBURGERSTRASSE 43A **TELEPHONE** NO
OPENING HOURS SUN-THU 12.00-01.00, FRI-SAT 12.00-04.00
CREDIT CARDS NONE **PRICE** € 2 **U-BAHNHOF** ORANIENBURGER TOR

You'll definitely pass this small roadside stall as you walk
down Oranienburgerstrasse. Don't walk by it though,
or you'll miss the best French fries in town. Even Dutch
people claim that you can't get better fries in Holland.
What's so special about them? Well, the fries are crisp
and hot, but Markus Becker's incredible sauces are
best of all. Have you ever had fries with guacamole?
Or with garlic? Or chilli? We have tried them all, and
they're all amazing.

As the name suggests, Matchmaker is a cozy spot for a truly romantic evening. Make sure not to walk in feeling overly hungry, though. This restaurant is a member of the "Slow Food Society of Berlin," the local chapter of the pan-European counter-movement against fast food. Dining here is an experience, but it can also be time-consuming. You'll feast on French and Mediterranean cuisine mixed with Californian cooking. Try the delicious Wiener Schnitzel, the marvelous spinach salad, or one of the interesting vegetarian plates. While sipping on one of the excellent wines, you'll soon begin to warm to the concept of "slow food."

Matchmaker
slow motion pleasures

AUGUSTSTRASSE 91 **TELEPHONE** 28 07 121
OPENING HOURS DAILY 18.00-01.00 **CREDIT CARDS** AMEX, VISA, MASTERCARD **PRICE** € 16
S-BAHNHOF ORANIENBURGER STRASSE OR **U-BAHNHOF** ORANIENBURGER TOR

In Greek mythology, Penthesileia was queen of the Amazons, a woman who stands for power and femininity. For Sylvia Müller and Anke Runge, the two designers of the Penthesileia label, the Amazon queen's attitude typifies their design concept. Their bags and backpacks express individuality and sensuality by using new shapes and colors. Some of their designs are so extravagant, they could easily pass for modernist sculptures, and in fact, from the Tucholskystrasse, the shop is easily mistaken for a gallery. If you'd like to have something eye-catching hanging off your shoulder, Penthesileia is the place to go to.

Penthesileia
where ever i lay my bag

TUCHOLSKYSTRASSE 31 **TELEPHONE** 28 21 152
OPENING HOURS MON–FRI 10.00-19.00, SAT 10.00-16.00
CREDIT CARDS NONE **S-BAHNHOF** ORANIENBURGERSTRASSE

Kamala
thai wonders

ORANIENBURGERSTRASSE 69 **TELEPHONE** 28 32 797
OPENING HOURS SUN–TUE 11.30-24.00, FRI–SAT 11.30-01.00
CREDIT CARDS AMEX, VISA, MASTERCARD **PRICE** € 9 **S-BAHNHOF** ORANIENBURGERSTRASSE

Kamala is one of the few places on busy Oranienburger Strasse where you will find calm and quiet. Located in a cozy, candle-lit basement, the restaurant is an ideal place for a rendezvous or romantic tryst. The kitchen offers a huge range of delicious Thai food at reasonable prices. Check out the spicy Thai curry for € 8.50, the 'hot pots' with either chicken or fish for € 9 or try some of the vegetarian plates. The friendly servers are always happy to recommend additional plates and variations, with guaranteed good results. In Mitte, where there are very few Thai restaurants, Kamala is truly a gem.

Culinaria Salumeria

forza italia

TUCHOLSKYSTRASSE 34 **TELEPHONE** 28 09 67 67
OPENING HOURS MON–FRI 10.00 TILL LATE, SAT, SUN 11.00 TILL LATE
CREDIT CARDS NONE **PRICE** € 9 **S-BAHNHOF** ORANIENBURGERSTRASSE

Located on the busy corner of Tucholskystrasse and August-strasse, the Culinaria Salumeria is where Mitte's art crowd and trendsetters go for late lunches. The menu contains various pasta dishes from € 7 to € 10, as well as salads and a scrumptious minestrone. Visitors often take a break here for a sandwich or a cappuccino after going to the Kunstwerke on Auguststrasse. In summer, you can sit outside on the terrace until the wee hours and watch the passers-by. If you prefer cooking at home, a huge selection of cheeses, antipasti, Italian meats and sauces are also available. The owners are not Italian, but they definitely know what it takes to come close to the original.

For fashion-conscious women, this shop is truly paradise on earth. Over the past 15 years, Sterling Gold's Michael Boenke has collected about 250,000 evening dresses, gowns, and cocktail dresses spanning more than 60 years of fashion. The best of these are lined up in perfect color coordination in his gold-painted shop. Hundreds of the most luxurious gowns hang here, all in mint condition and priced very moderately. For example, a knee-length, silver, sequined evening dress is only € 199. If you fall in love with something but it doesn't fit you perfectly, one of the shop's tailors will happily 'redesign' it for you. Definitely seek this place out.

Sterling Gold
first-class, second-hand

HECKMANNHÖFE, ORANIENBURGERSTRASSE 32 **TELEPHONE** 28 09 65 00
OPENING HOURS MON-SAT 12.00-20.00 **CREDIT CARDS** VISA, MASTERCARD
S-BAHNHOF ORANIENBURGERSTRASSE OR **U-BAHNHOF** ORANIENBURGER TOR

Jubinal
good vibes

TUCHOLSKYSTRASSE 34 **TELEPHONE** NO
OPENING HOURS DAILY 19.00-06.00
CREDIT CARDS NONE **S-BAHNHOF** ORANIENBURGER TOR

Jubinal is located on the busy corner of Tucholsky-Auguststrasse and is one of Mitte's most popular bars. It's the perfect place to start a night out or to finish one off. The ambience is kitsch-free Neo-seventies, the stereo plays downtempo and mixed drinks and cocktails are available for € 6 to € 8. On weekends, a live band plays classic jazz. Don't worry about the doorman; he's there to keep out the drunks, not you.

Essenbeck
pure fashion

AUGUSTSTRASSE 72 **TELEPHONE** 28 38 87 25
OPENING HOURS MON-FRI 12.00-20.00, SAT 12.00-18.00
CREDIT CARDS VISA, MASTERCARD **S-BAHNHOF** ORANIENBURGER TOR

Although Mitte is considered the trendiest area in Berlin, there are surprisingly few good fashion boutiques there. Essenbeck is one exception, carrying the more elaborate European designer labels exclusively for those in the know. You'll notice instantly that the selection of labels and garments is done by professionals; namely, the stylists, photographers and designers who run the place. Most of the labels are known for their functionality, and some for their classic elegance. You'll find clothing by names like Hussein Chayalan, Vexed Generation or Salia van Drimmelen. If these names mean nothing to you, that's because this is a store for dedicated followers of fashion!

Café Bravo

vegetarian snacks, contemporary art

🍴 AUGUSTSTRASSE 69 **TELEPHONE** 28 04 49 03 **OPENING HOURS** MON-THU 10.00-0.00,
SAT 10.00-02.00 **CREDIT CARDS** NONE **PRICE** SANDWICH € 4
S-BAHNHOF ORANIENBURGERSTRASSE OR **U-BAHNHOF** ORANIENBURGER TOR

Located inside Berlin's Institute for Contemporary Art, Café Bravo is one of Mitte's hottest spots. Inside a bright, glass pavilion (designed by American sculptor Dan Graham), it offers a great view into the backyard of Kunstwerke, where many international artists display their work. Kunstwerke is the venue for the Berlin Biennial, so if you're there at that time, you are almost guaranteed to see a famous artist at Café Bravo. In addition to the celebrities, there's also some very good food here, like a vegetarian English breakfast for € 8. The food is accompanied by great tunes, which, on weekends, are played by well-known Berlin DJs.

If you're into Motown, Soul, Ska and Gospel, Don De Lion is the perfect place for you. Located in the central square of Heckmann Höfe, which resembles a small Tuscan piazza, Don De Lion is both a Caribbean bar and record shop all in one. It's an interesting mix of rare vinyl and classic 60's music with a fine selection of drinks and finger food priced at € 3 to € 7. Grab a seat on one of its comfy lounge chairs and enjoy a Red Stripe or a well-stirred Margarita. And don't forget to flip through the record shelves - you might just find that Diana Ross record you've been looking for everywhere!

Don De Lion Bar

caribbean flavours

HECKMANN HÖFE, ORANIENBURGERSTRASSE 32 **TELEPHONE** 28 38 74 37
OPENING HOURS TUE-FRI FROM 19.00, SAT, SUN FROM 14.00
CREDIT CARDS NONE **PRICE** € 6 **S-BAHNHOF** ORANIENBURGERSTRASSE

Hut Up!
fashion for individualists

HECKMANN HÖFE, ORANIENBURGERSTRASSE 32 **TELEPHONE** 28 38 61 05
OPENING HOURS TUE-FRI 11.00-20.00, SAT 10.00-18.00
CREDIT CARDS NONE **S-BAHNHOF** ORANIENBURGERSTRASSE

Looking for unique hats that will keep you warm in winter and cool in summer? Then Hut Up! is the place for you. Whether it's a cocktail hat, Russian-style fleece cap or hat with attached dreadlocks, you'll find it here. The headgear is designed and manufactured by Christine Birkle in her small studio, located at the back of the shop. In addition to her handmade hats and caps, she also carries elegant clothing and beautiful bags made from fine Merino and wool from Irish, French or Mongolian sheep. In summer, Hut Up! also stocks lighter clothing tailored and designed with equal style and originality.

Oren is located right next to Berlin's most beautiful synagogue, at the edge of the old Jewish district. From inside the restaurant you can sometimes even catch a glimpse of the synagogue's golden dome reflected in the building opposite. Oren serves rich vegetarian food, from falafels to eggplant dishes, matzo bread and excellent fish, all at moderate prices. This is a great place for kosher delicacies and fine Israeli wines from the Golan Heights, Carmel and Barkan. The international atmosphere is unique, and for true vegetarians Oren is not to be missed. There are only a few restaurants that can compare!

Oren
kosher delicacies

ORANIENBURGERSTRASSE 28 **TELEPHONE** 28 28 228 **OPENING HOURS** MON-THU 12.00-01.00, FRI 12.00-02.00, SAT 10.00-02.00, SUN 10.00-01.00 **CREDIT CARDS** NONE **PRICE** € 8 **U BAHNHOF** ORANIENBURGER TOR OR **S-BAHNHOF** ORANIENBURGERSTRASSE

Double Happiness
japanese fine arts

 KRAUSNICKSTRASSE 6 **TELEPHONE** 28 09 77 41
OPENING HOURS MON–FRI 12.00-20.00
CREDIT CARDS NONE **S-BAHNHOF** HACKESCHER MARKT OR ORANIENBURGERSTRASSE

You eat sushi, you take pictures with Japanese cameras, and maybe
you even have a pair of those fancy Nippon jeans. So isn't it time to
explore how Japanese people actually live? Check out Double Happiness, where you can find the real thing; from Kimonos to wooden
shoes, to interior design items such as tatami mats, shoji sliding
screen doors, porcelain, paper lamps and even tea and incense sticks.
The people at Double Happiness will also advise you on where to find
good zen meditation courses. I think I'm turning Japanese!

Hasir

turkish for yummy

ORANIENBURGERSTRASSE 4 **TELEPHONE** 28 04 16 16 WWW.HASIR.DE
OPENING HOURS DAILY 12.00-01.00 **CREDIT CARDS** VISA, MASTERCARD **PRICE** € 13
S-BAHNHOF HACKESCHER MARKT OR **U-BAHNHOF** WEINMEISTERSTRASSE

A brand new branch of the legendary Turkish restaurant from Kreuzberg, Hasir Mitte is slightly more luxurious in every way. You'll notice it as you enter as the professional service staff welcome you and show you to your seat. To begin your meal, chose from typical Turkish starters, served like tapas on small plates. For your main course, priced at about € 12 to € 15, try one of the delicious grill-roasted lamb dishes. The servings are huge, so bring an appetite because at Hasir, the food is too good for left overs!

Riva Bar

thirtysomething

DIERCKSENSTRASSE 142 (UNDERNEATH THE S-BAHN ARCHES) **TELEPHONE** 24 72 26 88
OPENING HOURS DAILY 20.00-04.00
CREDIT CARDS VISA, MASTERCARD **S-BAHNHOF** HACKESCHER MARKT

The average age at Riva, a bar named for Italian soccer star Luigi Riva, is 35. If you're in this age group, or interested in people who are, this is the place to go. On weekend nights, admission is strict and you'll have to get past the bouncer at the door. If you're not up to this task, try a week night, when it should be easier to get in. Once inside, pull up a seat at the bar (shaped like an ocean liner), try a tasty cocktail and gaze at the colorful ceiling. You'll be surrounded by some of Berlin's rich and famous - or at least people who look like them.

From its roof to its basement, Haus Schwarzenberg is one of the few places in the gentrified area of Rosenthaler Strasse where the remnants of Berlin's once-thriving counter-culture still exist. On the upper levels there are artists' studios, while on the second floor is Neurotitan, the record shop that shares its space with an off-beat art gallery and a small book store. On the ground floor, Eschloraque is an exclusive bar open only to those who know the ever-changing password. The basement of the building houses Dead Chickens, an artist's collective known for their work in steel. Haus Schwarzenberg is one of the last remains of Mitte's glorious past, and definitely worth looking into!

Haus Schwarzenberg e.v.

an alternative hold-out

ROSENTHALERSTRASSE 39 **TELEPHONE** 30 87 25 73
OPENING HOURS MON-FRI 12.00-19.00, SAT 12.00-16.00
CREDIT CARDS NONE **U-BAHNHOF** HACKESCHER MARKT

Trippen Shop Berlin
these shoes are made for walking

HACKESCHE HÖFE, HOF 4 & 6, ROSENTHALERSTRASSE 40-41 **TELEPHONE** 28 39 13 37
OPENING HOURS MON-FRI 12.00-19.00, SAT 10.00-17.00
CREDIT CARDS VISA, MASTERCARD **S-BAHNHOF** HACKESCHER MARKT

Trippen is the only Berlin shoe brand that has made it on the international fashion scene. Founded in 1992, Trippen shoes soon became an insider tip for those bored with Italian styles. The secret to its success? The shoes are of a basic but unusual design, very comfortable and tend to last for ages. In Japan, Trippen is considered one of Europe's hippest shoe brands; so don't be surprised if you see many Japanese tourists around the store. If you don't mind slight production errors, check out the factory outlet on Chausseestrasse 35, where you might find some real bargains.

Hirafi
oriental living

SOPHIENSTRASSE 5 **TELEPHONE** 28 04 71 71
OPENING HOURS MON-FRI 12.00-19.00, SAT 11.00-18.00
CREDIT CARDS NONE **S-BAHNHOF** HACKESCHER MARKT

'Hirafi' is the Arabic word for an artisan, and arts & handicrafts from the Arab world are the focus of this small shop, which opened in late 1999, and is situated at the back of Hackescher Höfe. This is where you'll find classic Arab steel lamps, Moroccan ceramics, Tunisian terracotta, pots and pans, vases and dishes, and a good selection of Lebanese wine. It's also a great place for Turkish and Moroccan kelems - those wonderfully colorful, hand-knitted rugs. For unique middle-eastern interiors, Hirafi, is worth a visit.

Barcomi's

pure americana

SOPHIENSTRASSE 21 **TELEPHONE** 28 59 83 63
OPENING HOURS MON–SAT 09.00-22.00, SUN 10.00- 22.00
CREDIT CARDS NONE **PRICE** € 8 **S-BAHNHOF** HACKESCHER MARKT

The menu at Barcomi's reads: "We'd like to spoil you with American specialties and superb coffee." One is, indeed, amazed by the taste and quality of the food served at this "American" coffee shop. These are probably the best bagels in town, and if you are a fan of New York-style cheesecake, you must try Barcomi's. It's a taste you'll never forget! The well-selected range of quality coffees and superb teas from around the globe are also sure to satisfy. Barcomi's is the perfect place to start or end a tour of Mitte. But make sure you bring a little extra cash, as the good things in life are not always free.

Looking over the shelves of Whisky & Cigars, it's easy to see that this is a place for the real connoisseur. There are more than 280 whiskies from all over the world, plus rare brands of rum, hard-to-find cigarettes and a huge variety of exquisite cigars. Eva Siche-Schmidt, who runs Whisky & Cigars, will happily tell you about each product's origin in detail: where its ingredients come from, where it's made, where its stored and the best way to consume it. It's a real education, so take your time as you look around the store. For immediate gratification, there is even a small bar at which you can sample the products.

Whisky & Cigars

smoker's delight

SOPHIENSTRASSE 23 **TELEPHONE** 28 20 376 WWW.WHISKY-CIGARS.DE
OPENING HOURS TUE-FRI 12.00-19.00, SAT 11.00-16.00
CREDIT CARDS VISA, MASTERCARD **S-BAHNHOF** HACKESCHER MARKT

When the sun is out, Mitte's students and young adults hang out at Strandbad. Located in a cul-de-sac, deck chairs come out on the terraces as soon as the sun shines - no matter what the season. You can sit for hours watching young mothers play with their children in the nearby playground or sunbathe while sipping a 'café au lait'. Besides the quiet location, the Strandbad Mitte is also popular for its break-fast muesli, as well as its inexpen-sive and fresh salads. Don't be in a rush though...service here is very slow.

Strandbad Mitte
the sun always shines

KLEINE HAMBURGERSTRASSE 16 **TELEPHONE** 28 08 403
OPENING HOURS MON-SUN 09.00-02.00
CREDIT CARDS NONE **PRICE** € 6 **S-BAHNHOF** ORANIENBURGERSTRASSE

Claudia Skoda

original berlin fashion

LINIENSTRASSE 156 **TELEPHONE** 28 07 211
OPENING HOURS MON–FRI 12.00-19.00, SAT 13.00-18.00 **CREDIT CARDS** AMEX, VISA,
MASTERCARD **U-BAHNHOF** ROSENTHALER PLATZ OR ORANIENBURGER TOR

Berlin's fashion scene is not known for its inventiveness. For decades, only a few local labels have made it in the international market. One of these is Claudia Skoda, who has been designing knitwear for more than 25 years. In the 1980s, Skoda was so popular that she had her own shop in Manhattan. When the wall came down, she decided to return to her hometown and opened up her second shop in Berlin, here on Linienstrasse. This is where you'll find her colourful gowns, jackets and trousers, all knitted from different fabrics and presented in a tasteful, gallery-like ambience. If you are looking for an original souvenir with style, pay a visit to Claudia Skoda.

Andechser Hof

bavarian hospitality

ACKERSTRASSE 154 **TELEPHONE** 28 09 78 44 WWW.ANDECHSERHOF.DE
CREDIT CARDS AMEX, VISA, MASTERCARD **PRICE** FROM € 77
U-BAHNHOF ROSENTHALER PLATZ

"A little piece of Bavaria in the heart of Berlin." That's
the slogan of this hotel on quiet Ackerstrasse, and
indeed, the rooms are full of original Bavarian features
and Bavarian food and beer are served in the restaurant. The quality - by German standards - is basic but
the hotel is spotlessly clean, with showers or bathtubs
and a color TV in every room. Don't expect too much
from the service though. For what you get, the rates
could not be better. Single rooms are available for
€ 62, while a double room is available for € 77. A real
bargain considering its location.

While most of Berlin's fashion designers concentrate on the more functional aspects of clothing, Ayzit Bosnan focuses more on the classic cut. This is fashion that is not trendy, but modern. Made of the finest fabrics and with such timeless elegance, these clothes can hang in your wardrobe for years without looking dated. Consequently, Bosnan's small collection of dresses, blouses, jackets and leather bags draw fans from all over the continent. Also check out her line of accessories. This is a good opportunity to find something really unique and special.

Ayzit Bosnan
fashion

ACKERSTRASSE 154 **TELEPHONE** 27 90 87 94
OPENING HOURS MON–FRI 12.00-19.00, SAT 12.00-16.00
CREDIT CARDS NONE **U-BAHNHOF** ROSENTHALER PLATZ

75

Ultra-popular with the hip, young Mitte crowd, this bakery and snack bar offers tons of Portuguese delicacies. If you've been to Portugal, you likely fell in love with all these treats: Galaos, Bica, Portuguese wines, Sagres & Superbock. This is also a great place for sandwiches, tapas, panini and crab croquettes. In the colder months, try some delicious soups for just € 4. You'll enjoy good food and a friendly atmosphere while sitting at one of the window seats watching the world go by

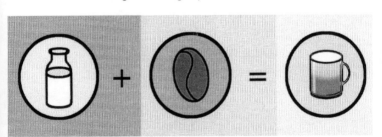

Galao
cool portuguese bakery

 WEINBERGSWEG 8 **TELEPHONE** 44 04 68 82
OPENING HOURS MON–FRI 08.00-20.00, SAT, SUN 10.00-18.00
CREDIT CARDS NONE **PRICE** € 3 **U-BAHNHOF** ROSENTHALER PLATZ

Vino e Libri
italian food, good books

TORSTRASSE 99 **TELEPHONE** 44 05 84 71
OPENING HOURS DAILY 18.00-01.00
CREDIT CARDS NONE **PRICE** € 13 **U-BAHNHOF** ROSENTHALER PLATZ

What a great combination: good books, well-selected wines and excellent Italian cooking. Surely this is what makes Vino e Libri one of the most popular Italian restaurants in Mitte. Make sure you reserve a table in advance, because this restaurant is always packed at dinnertime. You can choose from the romantic candle-lit tables at the back, or the tables in front where the atmosphere is more relaxed. Wherever you take your seat, you'll be assured of friendly and attentive service. Main courses are about € 13, which, considering the quality of the food, is a bargain.

Annachron
furniture and stuff

TORSTRASSE 93 **TELEPHONE** 01 79 69 66 251 WWW.ANNACHRON.DE
OPENING HOURS MON-FRI 14.00-19.00, SAT 13.00-17.00 **CREDIT CARDS** NONE
S-BAHNHOF HACKESCHER MARKT OR **U-BAHNHOF** WEINMEISTERSTRASSE

At Annachron, service is the top priority. As soon as you walk in the
door, you'll be greeted by a friendly sales person, who will offer you
champagne or coffee to make you feel as at home as in your own
living room. As you wander around the store, have a seat on one of the
colorful and comfy sofas, most from the early 60s, or check out one
of the wooden sideboards, which are also throwbacks of the past.
The products here are all old, but not old-fashioned, and are beautiful
in design. You'll almost always find something nice to add to your
home at Annachron, but if not, then just enjoy the friendly service.

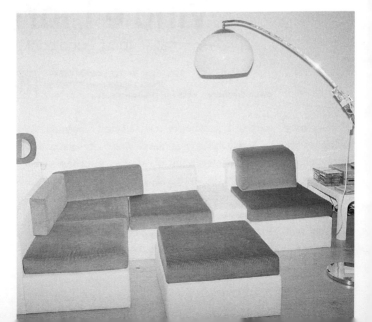

Hackbarths was one of the first cafés to open in trendy Mitte, in the early 90s. It's considered something of a classic, and luckily not swamped with tourists. Breakfast and warm quiches are served for less than € 6 until the afternoon, but most Mitte locals just come here to have a café au lait, chat and gossip a bit or read the newspaper. In the mornings, local art dealers from the near by Linienstrasse arrive for their first business meetings. On Sundays, Hackbarths is a meeting spot for young families from the neighborhood.

Café Hackbarths
coffee and quiches

AUGUSTSTRASSE 49A **TELEPHONE** 28 27 706
OPENING HOURS MON-THU 09.00-03.00 **CREDIT CARDS** NONE **PRICE** € 4
S-BAHNHOF ORANIENBURGERSTRASSE OR **U-BAHNHOF** ORANIENBURGER TOR

The name says it all: This is a restaurant serving Brazilian specialties (although it's not run by Brazilians). The atmosphere and the menu are close to the real thing, and give a genuine impression of the country. Media types, soap-stars and local hipsters dine here, enjoying an excellent range of hearty rump steaks, marinated fish, and bean and chili dishes. Unlike most meat-mad Brazilian restaurants, this one offers a selection of vegetarian plates from € 8 to € 15. If you're not too hungry, the impressive list of tequila and rum cocktails and the collection of cigars might whet your appetite. This is a good place to get a sense of the rich variety in Brazilian cuisine, but for the authentic item, you might want to look elsewhere.

Brazil
the grill from ipanema

GORMANNSTRASSE 22 **TELEPHONE** 28 59 90 26
OPENING HOURS DAILY 10.00-02.00 **CREDIT CARDS** VISA, MASTERCARD
PRICE € 13 **U-BAHNHOF** WEINMEISTERSTRASSE OR ROSENTHALER PLATZ

Blaues Band

good for breakfast

ALTE SCHÖNHAUSERSTRRASSE 7-8 **TELEPHONE** 28 38 50 99
OPENING HOURS DAILY 10.00-02.00 **CREDIT CARDS** VISA, MASTERCARD **PRICE** € 6
S-BAHNHOF HACKESCHER MARKT OR **U-BAHNHOF** ROSA-LUXEMBURG-PLATZ

The 'Blaue Band', or 'blue ribbon', is what great ocean liners were once decorated with. In this case, however, it's the cuisine that deserves the blue ribbon. The menu focuses on seafood, and is changed twice a week. Vegetarian dishes also abound, with a huge selection of delicious salads and meatless main courses. But the real attracions here are the pancakes, served Canadian-style, and available for € 5. In the summer, there's plenty of sunshine out on the terrace.

Pro Qm
thematic reading

ALTE SCHÖNHAUSERSTRASSE 48 **TELEPHONE** 24 72 85 20 WWW.PRO-QM.DE
OPENING HOURS MON-FRI 12.00-20.00, SAT 11.00-16.00
CREDIT CARDS VISA, MASTERCARD **U-BAHNHOF** ROSA-LUXEMBURG-PLATZ

Pro Qm (meaning 'per square meter') is a theme-oriented bookstore. Each month, the focus is on a different subject in the fields of urbanism, politics, pop-culture, architecture, design, art and theory. A special selection of books is available for each subject, and once or twice a week there are lectures and discussions in the back room. The store's regular stock is equally interesting, with a superb selection of German and international books plus a huge range of international magazines. You'll find everything from Wallpaper to Purple Prose, and from the Baffler to Frieze Magazine. Needless to say, Pro Qm is an essential store for anyone to check out - not just academic types.

For most men, finding good suits and casual wear is not an easy task. That's why we should all thank God for Herr von Eden. This treasure trove of a store, run by 21-year-old Ben Jensen, stocks new and second-hand suits, shirts and ties starting at € 100. Jensen has chosen the classiest cuts from the past 70 years - from three-piece suits to cool denim - and everything is in excellent condition. The only caveat is that the big man will have a hard time, as most of the suits are for men of average build.

Herr von Eden
men's clothing

ALTE SCHÖNHAUSERSTRASSE 7 **TELEPHONE** NO
OPENING HOURS MON-FRI 12.00-19.00, SAT 12.00-16.00 **CREDIT CARDS** NONE
U-BAHNHOF ROSA-LUXEMBURG-PLATZ OR WEINMEISTERSTRASSE

'Stue' is the Danish word for living room, and that's exactly what you'll find in this store. Every few months Marie Rädiker travels to Denmark to chose a new selection of furniture, lamps, ceramics and glass. The biggest names in Danish design are all here, but you'll also find many 'no name' items with equally timeless beauty. Everything is in such good condition that you'll be surprised to hear it's all second hand. And with these prices, you'll wish you had come to Berlin in a truck!

Stue
danish living

ALTE SCHÖNHAUSERSTRASSE 48 **TELEPHONE** 24 72 76 50
OPENING HOURS MON–FRI 14.00-19.00, SAT 13.00-17.00 **CREDIT CARDS** NONE
S-BAHNHOF HACKESCHER MARKT OR **U-BAHNHOF** WEINMEISTERSTRASSE

Monsieur Vuong

indochina mon amour

ALTE SCHÖNHAUSERSTRASSE 46 **TELEPHONE** 30 87 26 43
OPENING HOURS MON-SAT 12.00-24.00
CREDIT CARDS NONE **PRICE** € 7 **U-BAHNHOF** WEINMEISTER STRASSE

85

While sitting at the main table at Monsieur Vuong's, you'll notice a big black and white picture of a man with huge muscular arms smiling at you. This is Monsieur Vuong, father of the tiny restaurant's owner, Dat Vuong. This is one of Mitte's few Vietnamese restaurants, and for many people it's simply the best around. The Vietnamese salads and Won Ton soups, either vegetarian or with meat, are absolutely delicious and, at € 6.50, very reasonable. Have a Saigon beer or one of the restaurant's great teas to add the finishing touch to a delightful meal. Everything is made freshly, and you can even see the cooks at work. No wonder it's always busy at Monsieur Vuong's!

Blush

hot lingerie

ALTE SCHÖNHAUSERSTRASSE 25 **TELEPHONE** 42 02 27 01
OPENING HOURS MON–FRI 12.30-19.30, SAT 12.00-16.00 **CREDIT CARDS** MASTERCARD
S-BAHNHOF HACKESCHER MARKT OR **U-BAHNHOF** WEINMEISTERSTRASSE

Not only is this a well-chosen name for a store carrying those bits of a woman's wardrobe that set men on fire; the products that the store carries are carefully selected as well. Blush is not just about seduction, however. Owner Claudia Kleinert stocks a range of products - from underwear basics and nightgowns to a special range of beauty products and classy lingerie by exclusive Italian brands, as well as Blush's own label. Don't miss a visit to this shop - a woman's world where prices are affordable, service is friendly and the atmosphere comfortable.

Through the shop window, Macchina looks like a hardware store for coffee. Indeed, the store carries everything you need to make a perfect cup of coffee, Italian style. You'll find loads of espresso machines, chrome sugar tins, beautiful cups, automatic whisks that make milk soft and foamy and a variety of international coffees, varying in size, price and quality. Down the road at Neue Schönhauserstrasse 15, is Macchina's own café, the Espresso Bar, where you can check out the range of coffees sold in the store and watch the machines in action.

Macchina
mecca for caffeine addicts

ALTE SCHÖNHAUSERSTRASSE 26 **TELEPHONE** 28 38 44 14 WWW.MACCHINA-CAFFEE.DE
OPENING HOURS MON–FRI 10.00-19.00, SAT 11.00-15.00
CREDIT CARDS AMEX, VISA, MASTERCARD **U-BAHNHOF** WEINMEISTERSTRASSE

87

Authentics is part gallery, part store and full of interesting and well-designed home accessories. Every few weeks there is a small exhibition on subjects within the field of design, but on a daily basis people come here for the things they need for their home. You won't find trendy labels here, but you will find individualistic kitchen utensils, desk and bathroom accessories, featuring the brilliant ideas of some of Europe's young designers. Much of the merchandise is made of plastic, with some items in wood or felt, and it's all very tasteful and functional.

Authentics
functional interior design

ALTE SCHÖNHAUSERSTRASSE 19 **TELEPHONE** 28 09 92 92 WWW.AUTHENTICS-SHOP.COM
OPENING HOURS MON-FRI 12.00-20.00, SAT 11.00-16.00
CREDIT CARDS AMEX, VISA, MASTERCARD **S-BAHNHOF** HACKESCHER MARKT

Schönhauser
back to the present

NEUE SCHÖNHAUSERSTRASSE 17 **TELEPHONE** 28 11 704
OPENING HOURS MON-FRI 12.00-20.00, SAT 11.00-16.00 **CREDIT CARDS** NONE
S-BAHNHOF HACKESCHERMARKT OR **U-BAHNHOF** WEINMEISTERSTRASSE

Take a trip to the past at Schönhauser. If you're nostalgic for inflatable
sofas, psychedelic lamps and plastic tables you'll find your Mecca
here. The store is packed, so take time to wander around and gaze in
amazement at the huge collection. Most items date from the 30's to
the 80's, and are in mint condition. Prices were lower when Schönhauser
first opened a couple of years ago, but it's still possible to find good
second-hand gear at reasonable prices, and occasionally you'll even
find a bargain. Just on the off chance that you do score an amazing
deal, it's definitely worth checking this place out.

SUFF

spirits, wines, beers

NEUE SCHÖNHAUSERSTRASSE 16 **TELEPHONE** 28 57 143
OPENING HOURS MON-FRI 12.00-20.00, SAT 12.00-16.00
CREDIT CARDS NONE **S-BAHNHOF** HACKESCHERMARKT

'SUFF' means 'soaked' and it's the perfect name for a store specializing in things that will eventually get people tipsy. When entering, expect a warm welcome and friendly service. Don't be afraid to ask advice on the many types of beverages available. You'll find wines, beers, and various rums, whiskies and other hard liquors. The store even provides the best cure for a hangover - good, pure mineral water.

You can tell by the constant buzz of mobile phones in the air that Schwarzenraben is a hip spot. Indeed, it's frequented by many of Berlin's VIPs - actors, media mavens, politicians... you name it. With its high ceiling café, restaurant and small basement bar, this is one of the area's most popular spots. The restaurant serves excellent Italian/Mediterranean food and has an extensive wine list. Downstairs in the basement bar, well-stirred cocktails are on the menu. You might get lucky and meet a celebrity DJ here, since Schwarzenraben's owner also runs Berlin's top techno club, the Tresor.

Schwarzenraben
seeing and being seen

NEUE SCHÖNHAUSERSTRASSE 13 **TELEPHONE** 28 39 16 98 WWW.SCHWARZENRABEN.DE
OPENING HOURS DAILY 10.00-02.00 **CREDIT CARDS** AMEX, VISA, MASTERCARD
PRICE € 17 **S-BAHNHOF** HACKESCHER MARKT OR **U-BAHNHOF** WEINMEISTERSTRASSE

If you wear glasses, you know how hard it is to find a pair that looks good and improves your eyesight at the same time. Your problems may be solved at Brillenwerkstatt, which carries nearly 500 different frames in all shapes and sizes. They've got everything - from the most familiar brands to obscure and rare designer gear, and glasses made from the latest materials. Contact lenses and a huge variety of sunglasses are also available. If you don't find anything you like, you can design your own and Brillenwerkstatt will manufacture them for you (hence the name, which means 'glasses workshop').

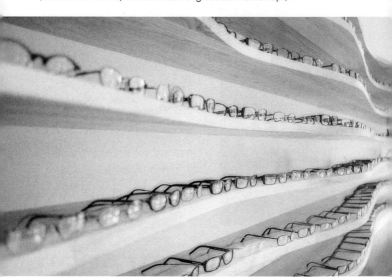

Brillenwerkstatt
the eyes have it

  DIRCKSENSTRASSE 48 **TELEPHONE** 28 09 67 40 WWW.BRILLENWERKSTATT.DE
OPENING HOURS MON-FRI 10.00-22.00, SAT 10.00-16.00
CREDIT CARDS AMEX, VISA, MASTERCARD **S-BAHNHOF** HACKESCHER MARKT

Honigmond Garden Hotel
green and quiet

INVALIDENSTRASSE 122 **TELEPHONE** 28 10 077 WWW.HONIGMOND-BERLIN.DE
CREDIT CARDS AMEX, VISA, MASTERCARD **PRICE** FROM € 100
U-BAHNHOF ZINNOWITZERSTRASSE

93

Located in a newly renovated, 19th-century house, the Honigmond Garden Hotel is one of the most romantic hotels in Mitte. Before the Berlin wall came down, the hotel's yard was a nursery, but now it's transformed into a serene, green oasis. If you're staying here, you'll find it a lovely place to chill out after a day of walking around Berlin. Chose a room with a garden view where in the evening you can hear birds singing. It's like being in the countryside, right in the center of Berlin. All rooms have attached bathrooms and are very reasonably priced: a single room costs € 65, a double, € 100. Check out the hotel's website for a first impression.

Alexander Plaza
celebrity hotel

 ROSENSTRASSE 1 **TELEPHONE** 24 00 10 WWW.ALEXANDER-PLAZA.COM
CREDIT CARDS AMEX, VISA, MASTERCARD **PRICE** FROM € 150
S-BAHNHOF HACKESCHER MARKT

The Alexander Plaza is just two minutes walk from Hackescher Markt, a popular spot for its shops, bars, cinemas and restaurants. Record companies regularly book rooms here, so don't be surprised if you bump into celebrities like Kruder & Dorfmeister, Beck or Oasis - they've all slept here. The rooms are comfortable, service is excellent and the hotel's bar well equipped. If you like to keep fit, there is a sauna and a small gym in the basement. The rates are appropriate to the hotel's standard and stature: € 140 to € 210 for a single room, € 10 extra for a double room. Breakfast is not included.

Although it might not to be considered beautiful, the Forum is full of history. Built in the early 60s, it was one of the leading East German hotels and was host to many of Eastern Europe's political elite. The rooms in the skyscraper are basic, but offer the best views you can get in any Berlin hotel. Rates go up as the floors go higher. € 175 will get you a single room on the 25th floor, € 200 for a double room, breakfast included. And note: the service at the Forum Hotel has its very own particular charm.

Forum Hotel
eastern standard

ALEXANDERPLATZ **TELEPHONE** 23 890 WWW.INTERCONTI.COM
CREDIT CARDS AMEX, VISA, MASTERCARD **PRICE** FROM € 200
U AND **S-BAHNHOF** ALEXANDERPLATZ

Riverside Hotel

rooms with a view

FRIEDRICHSTRASSE 106 **TELEPHONE** 28 49 00 WWW.TOLLES-HOTEL.DE
CREDIT CARDS VISA, AMEX, MASTERCARD **PRICE** FROM € 100
S-BAHNHOF FRIEDRICHSTRASSE

This small and charming hotel offers beautiful views. It's located alongside the river Spree, and from one of its double rooms, you can watch small boats sailing by. You'll see the Reichstag, and the Bertolt Brecht theatre, the Berliner Ensemble. Double rooms with a view range from € 130 to € 150, and are definitely worth the extra money. The single rooms don't have the same vistas, but a seat at the hotel's bar will provide an equally good view.

Reingold
lounge

NOVALISSTRASSE 11 **TELEPHONE** 28 38 76 76
OPENING HOURS SUN-THU 18.00-02.00, FRI-SAT 18.00-04.00
CREDIT CARDS VISA, MASTERCARD **U-BAHNHOF** ORANIENBURGER TOR

With its great art-deco ambience, reddish-brown lounge chairs and the famous portrait of classic German authors Klaus and Erika Mann at one end of the room, you could easily imagine yourself in Berlin in the 1920's. The age of Marlene Dietrich and Fritz Lang is still alive at Reingold. The crowd may be snooty, but the service and the drinks are excellent. Quality comes at a cost, however; be prepared to pay € 8 to € 10 for your perfectly made drink.

The stylish ambience at Kurvenstar looks like it's straight out of a 1970's B-movie and the crowd looks like it just came from a fashion shoot for The Face magazine. Kurvenstar is the bar where Mitte's hipsters meet. You can perch at the bar or on one of the comfy sofas in the back, where there's also a small dance floor for occasional partying. Cocktails and mixed drinks, priced at € 4 - € 8 are not as expensive here as elsewhere, but the atmosphere is cooler than in other places. Dress to impress.

Kurvenstar
seventies bar

KLEINE PRÄSIDENTENSTRASSE 3 **TELEPHONE** 28 59 97 10
OPENING HOURS SUN-THU 18.00-02.00, FRI, SAT 18.00-04.00
CREDIT CARDS VISA, MASTERCARD **S-BAHNHOF** HACKESCHER MARKT

Unfortunately, Berlin is not a city known for its bread making. There's the dry and tasteless roll called the 'Schrippe' and little dark rolls of rye called 'Schusterjungen', but that's about it with regards to breakfast. Thank heavens though for Marcann's, Mitte's best French bakery. They've got the freshest croissants, pain au chocolats and baguettes anywhere in the area, and everything tastes like it just came in from Paris. The truth is, you can watch everything being baked at Marcann's. Top the whole thing off with a cup of tea or a café au lait, and get a great start to your morning.

Marcann's
french bakery

INVALIDENSTRASSE 112 **TELEPHONE** 28 38 61 71
OPENING HOURS MON-FRI 07.00-18.00, SAT 10.00-16.00
CREDIT CARDS NONE **PRICE** SANDWICH € 3 **U-BAHNHOF** ZINNOWITZERSTRASSE

Lillibinär

ideal for a rendezvous

CHAUSSEESTRASSE 110 **TELEPHONE** 28 38 65 21
OPENING HOURS MON–FRI 11.30-02.00, SAT, SUN 17.00-02.00
CREDIT CARDS VISA, AMEX, MASTERCARD **PRIJS** € 7 **U-BAHNHOF** ZINNOWITZERSTRASSE

The Lillibinär is on Chausseestrasse, a street that is home to many of Berlin's dot-com companies. It seems almost out of place to sit inside this small and cozy restaurant and gaze at huge video projection screens in the building across the street. Lillibinär is urban with a 19th-century edge, serving Mediterranean food priced from € 6 to € 10. They play great lounge music, and have dimmed lighting, candles on the tables and dark velvet drapes hanging from the ceiling, providing a comfy and relaxed atmosphere. There's a mixed but not terribly trendy crowd, making Lillibinär quiet and down to earth; perfect for a rendezvous. If you're smart, you'll keep this your own little secret.

Donath
lazy sunday afternoons

SCHWEDTERSTRASSE 13 **TELEPHONE** 44 80 122
OPENING HOURS DAILY 10.00-01.00
CREDIT CARDS NONE **PRICE** € 7 **U-BAHNHOF** ROSENTHALER PLATZ

During the week you can easily find a spot at Donath, but weekends are a different story. The fantastic brunch buffet attracts hoards of hungry customers, who line up and wait for classic dishes such as salami Milanese, Parma ham, marinated zucchini and broiled eggplant. The fact that it faces the sun also makes Donath a great place to spend a lazy Sunday afternoon. If you feel like having a pizza, try the one with arugula; it's fantastic! The best thing about Donath is that you won't find too many tourists, since it's a little off the beaten track from both Mitte and Kollwitzplatz.

Art'Hotel
for the art lover

WALLSTRASSE 70-73 **TELEPHONE** 24 06 20
CREDIT CARDS VISA, MASTERCARD, AMEX
PRICE FROM € 148 **U-BAHNHOF** SPITTELMARKT

If you are an admirer of contemporary German art, this hotel is your number one choice. The whole hotel is like an exhibition of the work of Georg Baselitz, an icon of the 80's German art scene. Each room displays one of his paintings or drawings. Known for its friendly attitude towards artists, many curators, collectors and artists stay here when in Berlin for the art fair or the Berlin biennial. In addition, the atmosphere in the hotel is very friendly, the service good and the breakfast buffet extremely generous. Prices are appropriate for the hotel's standard: € 123 for a single, € 148 for a double.

Kreuzberg

Kreuzberg enjoyed its glory days during the 1980s, but life on Oranienstrasse, the area's main street, still bustles with a metropolitan feel. There are plenty of cafés, restaurants, bars and clubs worth visiting. Kottbusser Tor is the heart of Turkish Berlin, with many kebab houses, clubs, bars and Turkish travel agents. Every Tuesday and Friday there is an open-air Turkish Market along the Maybachufer, where you can get loads of fresh groceries and other ethnic specialties. A bit to the south is 'Kreuzberg 61' where, in the area around Bergmannstrasse, the atmosphere and energy of the '80s still lingers. The shops, restaurants and bars there haven't changed much since the Wall came down. South of Bergmannstrasse are many old houses that survived the bombings of World War II. For a glance of pre-war Berlin, visit the area around Chamissoplatz, which hasn't changed for more than a century.

Kreuzberg

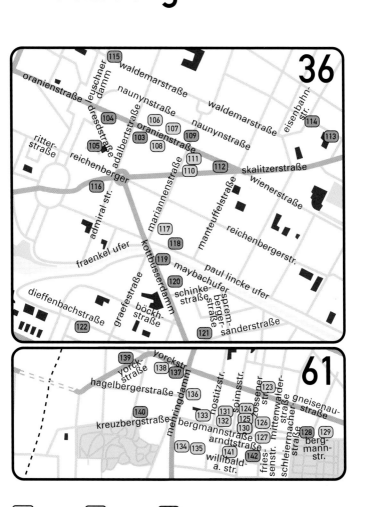

Legend has it that 'Döner Kebabs' (pockets of bread stuffed with roasted meat) were invented in Berlin by Turkish immigrants. Whether or not that is true, the Döner Kebab, along with currywurst, have come to be symbolic of Berlin's snack culture, and Hasir has the best döners in town. They are fresh, served with a special sauce and cost only € 2! Other Turkish delicacies, such as lamb with salad and böreks, are great too. Many Turks flood this restaurant day and night - a fantastic endorsement of how good, and authentic, the food is.

Hasir
the mother of all döners

ADALBERTRSTRASSE 10 **TELEPHONE** 61 42 373
OPENING HOURS DAILY 24 HOURS
CREDIT CARDS NONE **PRICE** € 5 **U-BAHNHOF** KOTTBUSSERTOR

You usually end up staying much longer at I Briganti than you had planned. The cozy place is a cross between a winery and snack bar, and has a few tables where you can rest and enjoy the excellent plates of cheese or bacon for € 6 to € 8, with a good bottle of wine. The main goal of the food here is not to fill an empty stomach, but more to give you a basis for your wine consumption. Prices are not bad, although you'd be surprised how quickly a bottle of wine disappears when it tastes this good.

I Briganti
small kitchen, big flavor

ORANIENSTRASSE 169 **TELEPHONE** 61 48 501
OPENING HOURS MON–SAT 11.00-22.00
CREDIT CARDS NONE **PRICE** € 8 **U-BAHNHOF** KOTTBUSSERTOR

Würgeengel
red, hot and cozy

DRESDENERSTRASSE 122 **TELEPHONE** 61 55 560
OPENING HOURS TUE-SUN 10.00-04.00, MON 16.00-04.00
CREDIT CARDS NONE **PRICE** € 8 **U-BAHNHOF** SCHÖNLEINSTRASSE

At Würgeengel the twenty and thirty-something's gather together to
drink, to snack and to flirt. Named after a film by Spanish director Luis
Bunuel, Iberian food is served here. Have a tapas plate with a glass of
Rijoa for € 10, or try the excellent spinach salad. If you are not hungry,
one of the well-stirred cocktails will provide you with equal joy. Be
patient finding a seat, the bar is very popular and always busy. But
for gazing at Kreuzberg's folks, you won't find a better place.

Melek Pastanesi

turkish-german bakery

ORANIENSTRASSE 28 **TELEPHONE** 61 45 186
OPENING HOURS DAILY 24 HOURS
CREDIT CARDS NONE **U-BAHNHOF** KOTTBUSSERTOR

Since Kreuzberg is an area with more immigrants than anywhere else in Berlin, it's quite natural that you find many ethnic shops here. addition to the scores of Turkish grocery stores, you'll also find places selling a more varied range of products. One of these is Melek Pastanesi, a bakery that sells both German and Turkish breads and sweets.

This store literally carries everything from 'Kraut' to 'Rüben' ('beets'). Specializing in eco-friendly products, the store is packed with fresh, organic fruits and vegetables, tofu products, juices, healthy bread and other foods that are good for you. Mothers who are conscious of feeding their children ecologically correct products, will surely find everything they need here. It's also the perfect supermarket for vegetarians and health nuts.

Kraut & Rüben
eco products

ORANIENSTRASSE 15 **TELEPHONE** 61 41 075
OPENING HOURS MON–FRI 09.00-18.00, SAT 09.00-14.00
CREDIT CARDS NONE **U-BAHNHOF** KOTTBUSSERDAMM

'Knofi' is German slang for 'Knoblauch', meaning 'garlic'. And that's exactly what you'll find in many fine pastes and sauces sold here. Check out things like humus and pesto, or try one of the delicious vegetarian salads, veggie burgers, antipasti, currant and seafood salad or couscous. Also delicious are the various coffee blends and pastas from Turkey and Italy.

Knofi
mediterranean delights

ORANIENSTRASSE 179 **TELEPHONE** 69 29 653
OPENING HOURS MON–FRI 11.00-20.00, SAT 09.00-16.00
CREDIT CARDS NONE **U-BAHNHOF** KOTTBUSSERTOR

Bateau Ivre

french café

ORANIENSTRASSE 18 **TELEPHONE** 61 40 36 59
OPENING HOURS SUN-THU 09.00-02.00, FRI, SAT 09.00-04.00
CREDIT CARDS NONE **PRICE** TAPAS € 7 **U-BAHNHOF** KOTTBUSSERTOR

Conceived as a French coffeehouse where Kreuzberg artists and locals could have a good, strong cup of coffee during the day, this place is now equally buzzing at night even though they only sell cold tapas (for € 7). It's more the friendly and flirtatious atmosphere that draws in the crowds. If you don't feel like eating tapas, try one of the excellent cakes... The pink grapefruit tart hits like a bombshell!

Grüne Papeterie

gifts and stationeries

ORANIENSTRASSE 196 **TELEPHONE** 61 85 355
OPENING HOURS MON-FRI 10.00-19.30, SAT 10.00-16.00
CREDIT CARDS NONE **U-BAHNHOF** KOTTBUSSERTOR

In the beginning, you could only buy Eco-friendly paper here, made from recycled paper. Now the range of products has broadened, though the focus is still on 'green paper': paper made from flowers, hand-scooped paper from Tibet or cardboard boxes. They also stock other paper related products such as blank photo books, handmade leather-goods for pens, inks and wrapping paper. The shop has really good prices, if you are looking for something to brighten up your stationery, check it out.

The shop is tiny, but stocks everything a passionate skateboarder needs to surf the city's concrete: boards, axes, shoes, shirts, pants and rolls, plus lots of other board-related accessories. If you aren't up for cruising the city streets, check out some of the 'fingerboard' products, perfect for 'desktop' skaters. If all this sounds like a foreign language, go into Search & Destroy, and ask. Someone there will explain it all to you.

Search & Destroy
board shop

ORANIENSTRASSE 198 **TELEPHONE** 61 28 90 64
OPENING HOURS MON-WED 12.00-19.00, THU, FRI 12.00-20.00, SAT 11.00-16.00
CREDIT CARDS NONE **U-BAHNHOF** SCHLESISCHESTOR

Amrit

indian excellence

 ORANIENSTRASSE 202-203 **TELEPHONE** 61 25 550
OPENING HOURS SUN-THU 12.00-01.00, FRI, SAT 12.00-02.00
PRICE € 7 **CREDIT CARDS** VISA, AMEX, MASTERCARD **U-BAHNHOF** GÖRLITZER BAHNHOF

You can smell the masalas and spices wafting from the Amrit kitchen even from a distance. This is one of the most popular restaurants in Kreuzberger since the food is great, the service is always friendly and the prices are just right. It's a bit too noisy for a romantic rendezvous, but on any other night this is the perfect choice. Reservations are recommended as it's always packed.

Whether you crave an 'Apfelstrudel' at noon or a giant Viennese Schnitzel at night, Jolesch has what you're looking for. Austrian cuisine has many pleasures to offer, and Jolesch is one of the best places to try them all. Famous for its top quality food, Viennese-style coffee-house atmosphere and charming service, the restaurant is always very busy and attracts people from every area of Berlin. Mornings, when you can score an amazing breakfast for just € 8, are the best times to find a seat without reservation (Kreuzbergers like to sleep in).

Jolesch
strudels and schnitzels

MUSKAUERSTRASSE 1 **TELEPHONE** 61 23 581
OPENING HOURS DAILY 10.00-01.00
CREDIT CARDS NONE **PRICE** € 12 **U-BAHNHOF** SCHÖNLEINSTRASSE

This place has attained cult-like status among Berlin's vegetarians. It's a total experience, as you eat strange vegetarian dishes with fantastic names while surrounded with blasphemous kitsch. Main courses start at € 12, and for those of you who can't live without some sort of meat on your plates, there are some fish dishes too.

Abendmahl
vegetarian temple

MUSKAUERSTRASSE 9 **TELEPHONE** 61 25 170
OPENING HOURS DAILY 10.00-01.00
CREDIT CARDS NONE **PRICE** € 15 **U-BAHNHOF** SCHÖNLEINSTRASSE

Henne
old berlin restaurant

LEUSCHNERDAMM 25 **TELEPHONE** 61 47 730
OPENING HOURS WED-SUN 19.00-01.00
CREDIT CARDS NONE **PRICE** € 9 **U-BAHNHOF** MORITZPLATZ

If you're dieting, think twice before going to Henne. A cozy, old Berlin restaurant, it serves heavily broiled or grilled meat dishes that are quite greasy. Dieters might be stuck with nothing but the Kraut salad. 'Henne' means 'hen', and it's possible to order up the namesake too. The birds come with crisp skin and a mayonnaise-soaked potato salad as a side dish. The food is not cheap, but it's all carefully prepared... The chickens are soaked in milk for two days before cooking! After your meal, have an Obstbrände. It's a fruit liqueur, and it will help you digest! Make sure to make a reservation.

Morgenland
breakfast dinner and lunch

SKALITZERSTRASSE 35 **TELEPHONE** 61 13 183
OPENING HOURS DAILY 10.00–01.00
CREDIT CARDS NONE **PRICE** € 6 **U-BAHNHOF** GÖRLITZER BAHNHOF

For a culinary tour of Germany, there's no better place than Morgenland. The café has a varied menu with the best choice from many different regions. If you're in the mood for northern food, try some of the North Sea fish. For a southeastern taste, try 'Maultasche', the Swabian equivalent of Italian ravioli. Drinks here are interesting as well, with different beers from the Rhine region, including 'Kölsch', and the famous 'Hefe-Weiße' from Bavaria. Prices at Morgenland are moderate and the food is always very good.

The shop is not easy to find, but if you keep looking you'll get there in the end. Follow the graffiti and stickers plastered on the walls to the second backyard, fourth floor. Hardwax is considered Berlin's best shop for electronic music. They've recently added dub and reggae records and CDs to otherwise extensive selection of house, techno and drum 'n' bass. All the latest releases are here, but there is also a huge section of rare and hard-to-find vinyl. For serious music-lovers, this place is a must.

Hardwax
electronic music shop

PAUL-LINCKE-UFER 44 **TELEPHONE** 61 13 01 11
OPENING HOURS MON-FRI 12.00-20.00, SAT 11.00-16.00
CREDIT CARDS VISA, MASTERCARD **U-BAHNHOF** KOTTBUSSERTOR

On Tuesdays and Fridays, when there's a market at Maybachufer, this café is the main meeting point for shoppers and sellers alike. One of Kreuzberg's oldest cafés, this is where many local people from the market enjoy their breakfast or snacks. In summer it's especially busy, and you can sit outside under a greenery-covered pergola. Breakfasts are available here from € 4 to € 8.

Café am Ufer
cozy riverside café

PAUL-LINCKE-UFER 42-43 **TELEPHONE** 61 22 827
OPENING HOURS MON-FRI 08.00-02.00, SAT, SUN 10.00-02.00
CREDIT CARDS NONE **PRICE** BREAKFAST € 6, LUNCH € 9 **U-BAHNHOF** KOTTBUSSERTOR

Ankerklause

riverside views

MAYBACHUFER 1 **TELEPHONE** 69 35 649 WWW.ANKERKLAUSE.DE
OPENING HOURS TUE-SUN 10.00-04.00, MON 16.00-04.00
CREDIT CARDS NONE **U-BAHNHOF** SCHÖNLEINSTRASSE

Small but busy, Ankerklause is one of the best places to enjoy a sunny day. Sit on the veranda of the bar with an Apfelschorle (apple juice with sparkling water) and watch the boats go by on the small canal. At night, chairs and tables are occasionally moved to make room for dancing. A CD player provides a constant and appropriate soundtrack, and snacks or a basic breakfast are served until late afternoon.

Musashi

japanese food

KOTTBUSSER DAMM 102 **TELEPHONE** 69 32 042
OPENING HOURS MON-SAT 12.00-22.30, SUN 14.00-22.00
CREDIT CARDS NONE **PRICE** SUSHI € 4 **U-BAHNHOF** SCHÖNLEINSTRASSE

Musashi serves some of the best sushi and Miso soup
in Berlin. Everything tastes super-fresh, and special
dishes can be made on request. Prices are good too...
Weekly specials, including soup and sushi, are less than
€ 5. Another nice thing about Musashi is the classical
music that is always playing

Soul Trade is the premier store in Berlin for contemporary dance music. It offers a diverse mix, heavy on Hip Hop, but also including old Soul, Jazz and Funk as well as modern electronic variants such as Drum 'n' Bass, House and Garage. You'll mostly find vinyl, but there is also a CD section. New stock comes in on Tuesdays and Thursdays, so those are the best days to go in terms of selection. While you're there you might run into one of the guys from Berlin's famous Jazzanova group... they used to work there before becoming professional DJs.

Soul Trade
contemporary dance music

SANDERSTRASSE 29 **TELEPHONE** 69 45 257 WWW.SOULTRADE.DE
OPENING HOURS MON-WED 11.00-19.00, THU, FRI 11.00-20.00, SAT 11.00-16.00
CREDIT CARDS AMEX, MASTERCARD **U-BAHNHOF** SCHÖNLEINSTRASSE

Pow-Wow is one the two hippest places in Kreuzberg to hang out (the other is Würgeengel). In the early 90s it was the capital of the grunge scene, but now it's more of a mixed, but young, crowd. They all come here for the yummy American comfort food. The meaty hamburgers (€ 7) are highly recommended, as are the desserts and cakes. Vegetarians can try the soy burgers, which are also very good.

Pow-Wow
young at heart

DIEFFENBACHSTRASSE 11 **TELEPHONE** 69 45 606
OPENING HOURS SUMMER DAILY 14.00-03.00, WINTER DAILY 17.00-03.00
CREDIT CARDS NONE **PRICE** € 8 **U-BAHNHOF** SCHÖNLEINSTRASSE OR SÜDSTERN

Radio Art

antique radios

ZOSSENERSTRASSE 2 **TELEPHONE** 69 39 435
OPENING HOURS TUE-FRI 13.00-18.00, SAT 10.00-13.00
CREDIT CARDS NONE **U-BAHNHOF** GNEISENAUSTRASSE

123

Radio may not play as important a role in people's lives as it once did, but it's still an important and worthwhile form of media. At least Horst-Dieter Schmahl thinks so... He owns Radio Art and has a collection of dozens of old radios and other electronic devices. As an engineer, he knows how to repair them, and would be happy to fix just about anything you bring him. The store is a fascinating place to browse and is somewhat of a survey of 60 years of broadcasting.

Tatau Obscur

tattoos, piercings and body art

SOLMSSTRASSE 35 **TELEPHONE** 69 44 42 88
OPENING HOURS MON–FRI 13.00-19.00, SAT 13.00-17.00
CREDIT CARDS NONE **U-BAHNHOF** GNEISENAUSSTRASSE

Some people are fascinated with applying
permanent ink to their body or altering the
shape of their ears, lips, nose and other body
parts. If you are one of those people, check out
Tatau Obscur, one of the best tattoo parlors in
Berlin. Owner Berit Uhlhorn is an artist, and you
have to see her work to believe it. If your tastes
run to the less permanent, Uhlhorn will adorn
you with a Henna tattoo.

Raw Musique

pure electronic music

ZOSSENERSTRASSE 20 **TELEPHONE** 69 47 815
OPENING HOURS MON-WED 13.00-20.00, THU, FRI 12.00-20.00, SAT 12.00-16.00
CREDIT CARDS NONE **U-BAHNHOF** GNEISENAUSTRASSE

Other than Hardwax, Raw Musique is the finest place in the city for electronic music. The two neighbouring stores carry all genres of music, whether it's House, Techno, Drum 'n' Bass, Downtempo or Experimental Electronica. The store on the right stocks new releases, while the one on the left has 90s music and rare vinyl and CDs. Don't be afraid to ask if you have questions...the guys behind the counter know everything. Just hum the melody of an old Aphex Twin song and they'll direct you straight to it.

Grober Unfug

comics & cartoons

ZOSSENERSTRASSE 32-33 **TELEPHONE** 69 40 14 90
WWW.HOME.T-ONLINE.DE/HOME/GROBERUNFUG **OPENING HOURS** MON-FRI 11.00-19.00,
SAT 11.00-16.00 **CREDIT CARDS** VISA, AMEX, MASTERCARD **U-BAHNHOF** GNEISENAUSTRASSE

Comics are king at Grober Unfug. This is the biggest
comic store in Berlin, and has just about everything.
The employees are extremely knowledgeable, and
will tell you exactly what titles are available for any
character you mention. The store also carries a large
assortment of paraphernalia for science fiction fans,
including Star Wars, Star Trek and Aliens merchandise.
There are also regular exhibitions, where cartoonists
come to sign their work.

Berlin ist Krimistadt

Hammett
crime novel shop

FRIESENSTRASSE 27 **TELEPHONE** 69 15 834 WWW.PARKVERBOT.ORG/HAMMETT
OPENING HOURS MON-FRI 11.00-20.00, SAT 11.00-15.00
CREDIT CARDS NONE **U-BAHNHOF** GNEISENAUSTRASSE

Fans of crime fiction will love this store. Hammett stocks over 5000 crime titles in German, and over 1000 in English. For collectors, the second-hand section has more than 2000 titles and includes some real rarities. Claudia Denker, the store's owner, is a crime fiction addict and will easily be able to help you out if you've forgotten the name of a title or author. Check out the store's website to see what's in stock.

Schnitzel in Vienna is like nothing else; thin, with a crispy crumb coating and about as big as a small pizza. And at Austria, they know how to do it just right. If you're feeling hungry, order the regular portion. If not, get the children's portion, which is still huge. While dining under deer's antlers, you'll feel like you are in the Austrian mountains. The cozy restaurant also serves very good Austrian and Bohemian food, in addition to the delicious schnitzels.

Austria
the schnitzel waltz

BERGMANNSTRASSE 30 **TELEPHONE** 69 44 440
OPENING HOURS DAILY 18.00-01.00
CREDIT CARDS NONE **PRICE** € 13 **U-BAHNHOF** GNEISENAUSTRASSE

Modulor
total material

GNEISENAUSTRASSE 43-45 **TELEPHONE** 69 03 60 WWW.MODULOR.DE
OPENING HOURS MON–WED 13.00-20.00, THU, FRI 12.00-20.00, SAT 12.00-16.00
CREDIT CARDS NONE **U-BAHNHOF** GNEISENAUSTRASSE

Architects, furniture designers and graphic artists are just some of the many people who turn their ideas into reality with supplies bought at Modulor. The store's catalogue is as thick as a phone book, and students at Berlin's design schools consider it and essential reference guide. Modulor is unique not only in Berlin, but also in the rest of Germany, a fact which is reinforced by one look at the license plates on the cars parked out front. People come from great distances to buy their material here. Check out the website for an impression of what it has to offer.

Whether in the kitchen or the workshop,
a good knife makes every job much easier.
Holzapfel stocks Japanese hand-made
knifes for every purpose, as well as saws,
blades and axes. These are top-of-the-line
tools for the avid craftsman or cook. If you
need the highest quality cutting tools, you'll
find them at Holzapfel.

Holzapfel
fine tools

BERGMANNSTRASSE 25 **TELEPHONE** 78 99 06 10
OPENING HOURS MON–FRI 11.30-19.00, SAT 11.00-14.30
CREDIT CARDS NONE **U-BAHNHOF** GNEISENAUSTRASSE

Aquamarin
jewelry and fountains

SOLMSSTRASSE 30 **TELEPHONE** 69 33 440
OPENING HOURS MON–FRI 12.00-19.00, SAT 11.00-15.00
CREDIT CARDS NONE **U-BAHNHOF** GNEISENAUSTRASSE

131

Aquamarin certainly has a unique concept. It sells jewelry and indoor fountains. Although it sounds like an odd combination, it makes sense as you stroll through the store. Some of the fountains, by Michael Kemmerling, actually look like liquid jewels, and the Lucie Schnurrer's jewelry occasionally takes the shape of waves. Other jewelry designers are represented here as well, along with the work of some young goldsmiths.

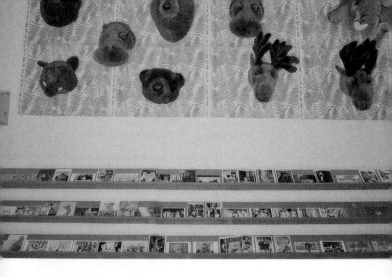

Ararat

postcards, stationery and gifts

BERGMANNSTRASSE 99A **TELEPHONE** 69 35 080
OPENING HOURS MON–FRI 10.00–20.00, SAT 10.00–16.00
CREDIT CARDS NONE **U-BAHNHOF** ZOSSENERSTRASSE

A couple of years ago, you could only find
postcards at Ararat. Now the range of
products has extended to include stationery
and small gifts. Postcards are still the main
draw here, however. Film and music celebrities have their own racks, and there are
many other categories of cards. For years,
Madonna, Elvis and Marilyn Monroe were
the biggest stars, but now you'll inevitably
find lots of Britney Spears and Robbie
Williams as well.

Bella Donna
beauty store

BERGMANNSTRASSE 101   **TELEPHONE** 69 48 323
OPENING HOURS MON–FRI 10.00-19.00, SAT 10.00-16.00
CREDIT CARDS AMEX   **U-BAHNHOF** GNEISENAUSTRASSE

133

Finding cosmetics made from natural ingredients is a lot easier than it used to be, but it's still good to know that there is a place like Bella Donna. In addition to beauty products of all kinds, the store carries essential oils and scents, baby clothes and beauty accessories. It's an ideal store for young mothers, or for beautiful women who want to become even more beautiful. Men, however, should probably wait in one of the nearby cafés.

In Bestform
kitchen and bathroom

BERGMANNSTRASSE 8 **TELEPHONE** 69 40 399 WWW.INBESTFORM.DE
OPENING HOURS MON–WED 10.00-19.00, THU, FRI 10.00-19.30, SAT 10.00-15.00
CREDIT CARDS AMEX **U-BAHNHOF** GNEISENAUSTRASSE

In Bestform is all about looking good. It's a wealth of interior design possibilities and items for the kitchen and bathroom. There are hundreds of styles of glassware, vases and pottery, and kitchen utensils made of steel, glass and plastic. There is so much here, it's impossible just to name a few items. But rest assured, no matter what your taste is there will always be something here that will look good in your home.

Hof-Atelier
fashion and bags

BERGMANNSTRASSE 105 **TELEPHONE** 69 40 13 98
OPENING HOURS MON-FRI 11.00-19.00, SAT 10.00-16.00
CREDIT CARDS VISA, MASTERCARD **U-BAHNHOF** MEHRINGDAMM

135

The Hof-Atelier is located in one of the hard-to-find
backyards that Kreuzberg is famous for. When located, these little hidden treasures often surprise you
with their beauty and quietness. This is a fashion
boutique for romantic and down-to-earth people,
carrying brightly colored clothing that's well designed
but not trendy. In addition, there are bags of different
shapes and sizes, as well as rings, beads and even
hammocks! It's a real find.

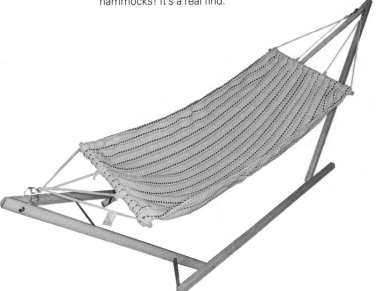

Faster, Pussycat!

second hand shop

MEHRINGDAMM 55 **TELEPHONE** 69 50 66 00
OPENING HOURS MON-FRI 11.00-19.00, SAT 11.00-16.00
CREDIT CARDS NONE **U-BAHNHOF** MEHRINGDAMM

Fancy a change of hairstyle? Skip a visit to your regular hairdresser and check out "Faster! Pussycat". Here they stock the most beautiful wigs, from afros to suicide blondes, all lengths, and colors are available. If you would like to add some extra spice to your wardrobe, check out the fashion in stock, a special selection of clothes and accessories from the 60's and 70's is available. Not to mention the tiled floor, the furniture and the lamps that give the shop a warm atmosphere.

The British cuisine is not what you could call world famous for it's delicacies, there's one dish that everyone fancies once in a while; its fish 'n chips. At the snack bar with the same name, you'll find this greasy specialty in many different variations. Of course, vinegar is available in different flavors plus additions such as scotch eggs or mushy peas. To complete your meal, have a cider or ale on the side.

Fish 'n Chips
british snack bar

YORCKSTRASSE 15 **TELEPHONE** 21 75 54 40
OPENING HOURS DAILY 12.00-01.00
CREDIT CARDS NONE **PRICE** € 6 **U-BAHNHOF** MEHRINGDAMM

Located in a former customs house, right on the corner between Kreuzberg and Schöneberg, the Exil is a design-shop for an extravagant taste. All that is sold here has something special about it. Be it the shape, color or the offbeat materials of which the chairs, sofas, lamps or tables are made, this shop is about the funky things in life. They don't come cheap though, but it's all very tasteful with an individualist edge.

Exil Wohnmagazin
extravagant interior designs

YORCKSTRASSE 24 **TELEPHONE** 21 73 61 90
OPENING HOURS MON–FRI 11.00-19.00, SAT 10.00-15.00
CREDIT CARDS NONE **S-BAHN** YORCK STRASSE

E.T.A. Hoffmann
fine foods

YORCKSTRASSE 83 **TELEPHONE** 78 09 88 09
OPENING HOURS MON-SAT 18.00-02.00
CREDIT CARDS VISA, AMEX, MASTERCARD **PRICE** € 30 **U-BAHNHOF** MEHRINGDAMM

There have been many new restaurant foundations in Berlin in recent years and this new breed has opened the city up to real gourmet pleasures. Amongst one of the new food temples is the E.T.A. Hoffmann. It's been mentioned in many restaurant guides for it's cozy atmosphere but it's mainly the restaurant's kitchen produce that make this place so special. Very simple ingredients are skillfully transformed into excellent cuisine. It's in the same league as the restaurants around the area of Gendarmenmarkt, but much cozier and the service is not as arrogant.

Osteria No.1

italian mothership

  KREUZBERGSTRASSE 1 **TELEPHONE** 78 69 162
OPENING HOURS DAILY 12.00-02.00
CREDIT CARDS VISA, AMEX, MASTERCARD **PRIJS** € 13 **U-BAHNHOF** MEHRINGDAMM

In Kreuzberg, it's one of the most popular
Italian restaurants. They are probably not
lying when they call themselves No.1. In
the eighties, early nineties the food used
to be even better, now it's still okay, but
portions are not so large, so make sure you
order different piattis if you are really hungry.
In summer, you can sit outside in a beautiful
garden, 'giardino from 20 degrees celsius'
is written on the menu.

For decades, the South Africa 's have been known for their fruits, only recently and especially since the fall of apartheid, its wines and food culture has become more and more popular. The Rigami has a good variety of South African wines from different vines in stock, plus cigars and anything and everything for a good picnic. In the back room there's a small bar where occasionally wine-testings are held, ask in the shop for further details. It's recommended to call before visiting the shop, the opening hours change quite often.

Rigami
south african wines and specialties

CHAMISSOPLATZ 5 **TELEPHONE** 69 41 260
OPENING HOURS TUE-FRI 14.00-20.00, SAT 11.30-16.00
CREDIT CARDS NONE **U-BAHNHOF** ZOSSENERSTRASSE

Amazingly, in the area of Kreuzberg 61 there aren't too many shops around that sell Italian delicacies. Why, is hard to explain, but thank goodness for the Il Ghiottone where you can get all the fine things that make the Italian cuisine taste so good: Wine, pasta, olive-oil, antipasti, salsas and pastry. At lunchtime, different plates are on offer for less than € 6 and if you are in a rush, you can even take them right away.

Il Ghiottone
italian specialties

ARNDSTRASSE CORNER FRIESENSTRASSE **TELEPHONE** 01 73 80 18 587
OPENING HOURS MON-FRI 10.00-19.30, SAT 10.00-14.30
CREDIT CARDS NONE **PRICE** € 6 **U-BAHNHOF** GNEISENAUSTRASSE

Schöneberg

A rich mixture of alternative lifestyle and up-market culture characterizes the borough of Schöneberg. Its bars and restaurants are attractive, and other than Kreuzberg, this is the best area for unique and offbeat shopping. Northwest of Nollendorfplatz, is Berlin's gay area, Motzstrasse, where many clubs and bars are to be found. Winterfeldstrasse has many antique bookshops as well as bars and restaurants open until the early hours of the morning. Just about anything and everything is sold at the twice-weekly market on Winterfeldtplatz. Further along is Goltzstrasse, which has the flair of New York's East Village, with many cafés and restaurants. On sunny days, the sidewalk cafes make Goltzstrasse seem like one big catwalk. Akazienstrasse is well known for its cozy restaurants, and just a few minutes away you will find the Rathaus Schöneberg where, in 1963, John F. Kennedy declared that he was "ein Berliner"!

Schöneberg

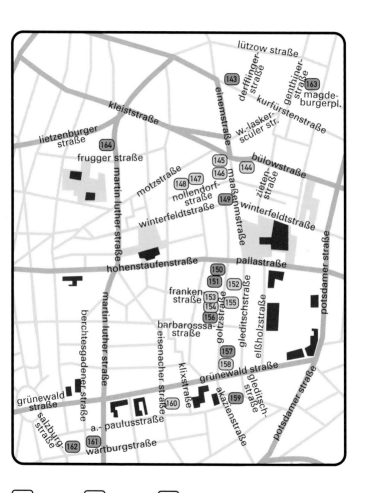

lützow straße

derfflinger straße

genthiner straße

(143)

(163)

magdeburgerpl.

kurfürstenstraße

kleiststraße

einemstraße

w.-lasker-schüler str.

lietzenburger straße

(164)

frugger straße

bülowstraße

motzstraße

(145)

(144)

(148) (147)

(146)

nollendorfstraße

maaßenstraße

zietenstraße

(149)

winterfeldtstraße

winterfeldtstraße

martin luther straße

hohenstaufenstraße

pallastraße

(150)

(151)

(152)

franken straße

(153)

(154) (155)

gleditschstraße

elßholzstraße

potsdamer straße

(156)

barbarosssastraße

golzstraße

(157)

(158)

eisenacher straße

berchtesgadener straße

martin luther straße

grünewald straße

gleditschstraße

(159)

klixstraße

akazienstraße

grünewald straße

(160)

potsdamer straße

salzburg straße

(162) (161)

a.- paulusstraße

wartburgstraße

Café Einstein
viennese coffeehouse

KURFÜRSTENSTRASSE 58 **TELEPHONE** 26 15 096
OPENING HOURS DAILY 10.00-2.00
CREDIT CARDS AMEX, VISA, MASTERCARD **PRICE** € 10 **U-BAHNHOF** NOLLENDORFPLATZ

Café Einstein is arguably the most beautiful Viennese coffeehouse in Berlin. Located in a well-tended 19th-century villa, it has a huge garden and a menu with everything a true Viennese coffeehouse should offer: coffee mélange; excellent white wines, 'Wiener Schnitzel' and 'Palatschinken'. You'll really feel like you're in Vienna and what's more, the waiters here are just as arrogant as they are in the Austrian capital! Prices are high, but worth it for the quality of the food and the beautiful surroundings. The German academic exchange service (DAAD) has its art gallery on the floor above the café. At openings of new shows there are bound to be lots of promising Berlin artists at the café.

Mr.Dead and Mrs.Free

uk and us music imports

BÜLOWSTRASSE 5 **TELEPHONE** 21 51 449
OPENING HOURS MON–WED 11.00-19.00, THU, FRI 11.00-20.00, SAT 11.00-16.00
CREDIT CARDS VISA **U-BAHNHOF** NOLLENDORFPLATZ

It is a sad fact that record players are harder and harder to find these days, but shops like Mr. Dead and Mrs. Free keep the vinyl culture alive, ensuring that the exchange of round plastic discs will never die out. Looking for that obscure 7″ single by Beck that was only released in Ireland? You'll find it here, along with the latest in brand-new releases from the UK and the US. The store also stocks a wide assortment of new Berlin rock and electronic-school from labels such as Kitty-Yo and Fucky. Rock on! And help save vinyl.

'Zapato' is the Portuguese word for shoes, and it's in Portugal that a brand of shoes with that name is manufactured. Most of the styles are classic, but some have a pointed shape rarely seen these days. Zapato has a small but good range of sandals and boots, sporty shoes and classical crêpe soles for sale. Most follow current trends, but don't expect to find any big names here. These shoes are all about comfort and individuality.

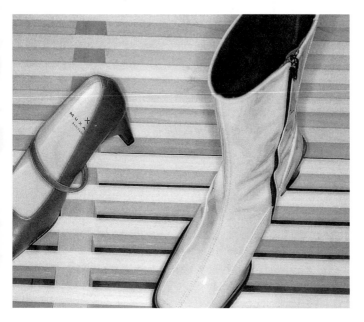

Zapato
shoes for him and her

MAASSENSTRASSE 14 **TELEPHONE** 23 62 98 91
OPENING HOURS MON-FRI 10.00-20.00, SAT 10.00-16.00
CREDIT CARDS VISA, AMEX, MASTERCARD **U-BAHNHOF** NOLLENDORFPLATZ

At Nettchen's fine bakery, pastry and art go together as well as the delicious, homemade croissants with a cup of coffee. On the walls is the work of Daniel Cinelli, a local artist who is well known for his concept of "Dump Art". These mostly "cut 'n' paste" pieces, are not what you would call extravagant, but they are all available for the modest sum of € 15. So after you've tasted some of the baked delicacies, why not add a piece of "Dump Art" to your private collection? You'll take away a good souvenir from Berlin, and every time you look at it, you'll remember the delicious pastries.

Nettchen's
art croissanterie

MAASSENSTRASSE 13 **TELEPHONE** 21 75 29 05
OPENING HOURS MON-FRI 07.00-18.00, SAT 07.00-16.00
CREDIT CARDS NONE **PRICE** SANDWICH € 2 **U-BAHNHOF** NOLLENDORFPLATZ

146

Kaukab
world music

NOLLENDORFSTRASSE 28 **TELEPHONE** 78 51 680
OPENING HOURS MON–WED 11.00–18.00, THU, FRI 11.00–19.00, SAT 11.00–16.00
CREDIT CARDS NONE **U-BAHNHOF** NOLLENDORFPLATZ

Explore the rich tradition of Arab musical culture at Kaukab, a world
music store focusing on the regions of North Africa to the Gulf States.
The store's name is borrowed from Oum-Kalthoun, a singer nicknamed
the 'Star of the Orient' ('Kaukab' means 'star'). This is the place for
tickets to Arabic music concerts, belly dances as well as information
on the Arab music scene in Berlin. If you prefer Cajun, Merengue or
Afro-Cuban music, you'll also find that here. This is a shop for real
music lovers.

Vinos Y Tapas

spanish wines and delicacies

NOLLENDORFSTRASSE 15 **TELEPHONE** 21 53 415
OPENING HOURS MON-FRI 12.00-19.00, SAT 10.00-15.00
CREDIT CARDS VISA, MASTERCARD **U-BAHNHOF** NOLLENDORFPLATZ

148

With two branches in former East Berlin, Vinos Y Tapas is one of
the most successful shops for Spanish delicacies and wines in Berlin.
On offer are specialties from all over Spain, from the light Andalusian
Manilas to the strong red wines of North Spain and Manchego cheese
from Toledo. The shop has all the food and ingredients that we know
and love Spain for. Olive oil, sherry, cavas and a massive range of wines
are available. Naturally, Spanish is spoken here. Olé!

Looking for a taste of the North? Located at the corner where the Winterfeldtmarkt is held every Saturday, Tim's Canadian Deli is the ideal place for dinner or just a quick snack after strolling through the market. Feast on turkey or spare ribs, try a vegetarian meal, or grab some French toast, bagels or a slice of one of dozens of Tim's cakes. Everything is fresh and delicious, and for real Canadian flavor, pour some maple syrup over your food. Some say it goes well with anything!

Tim's Canadian Deli
maple syrup and other fine things

MAASSENSTRASSE 14 **TELEPHONE** 21 75 69 60
OPENING HOURS MON–SAT 08.00-01.00, SUN 09.00-24.00
CREDIT CARDS AMEX, VISA, MASTERCARD **PRICE** € 7 **U-BAHNHOF** NOLLENDORFPLATZ

Pranzo e Cena

original neapolitan pizza

GOLTZSTRASSE 32 **TELEPHONE** 21 63 514
OPENING HOURS DAILY 12.00-01.00 **CREDIT CARDS** AMEX, VISA, MASTERCARD
PRICE PIZZA FROM € 6 **U-BAHNHOF** EISENACHERSTRASSE

Diehard pizza fanatics say Southern Italian style is the
only way to have pizza. These are not always easy to
find, but at Pranzo e Cena (meaning 'lunch and dinner'),
all your pizza fantasies will be fulfilled. Made of thin,
crispy dough topped with delicious tomato sauce and
olive oil, the pizza is baked in a traditional stone oven.
The menu also includes fresh homemade pasta, and
a list of wines from Southern Italy. For pizza and
pasta-lovers, it's a dream come true.

Café M

a berlin classic

GOLTZSTRASSE 33 **TELEPHONE** 21 67 092
OPENING HOURS MON-THU 08.00-02.00, FRI, SAT 09.00-03.00, SUN 09.00-02.00
CREDIT CARDS NONE **PRICE** € 4 **U-BAHNNHOF** EISENACHERSTRASSE

Café M has been around for almost two decades but it's one of the few classic Berlin spots that have made it well into the new millennium. In the 80s it used to be the one alternative bar everyone went to. Now European techno beats are all that can be heard. Although times may have changed, it's still crowded with Schöneberg's 20- and 30-somethings, plus loads of local talent. Breakfast is served, as well as snacks, but most of all you come to Café M to drink. The bar has a good range of beer and long drinks on the menu. In summer, sit outside and watch the world pass by on Goltzstrasse.

Das Alte Bureau
second hand office furniture

 GOLTZSTRASSE 18 **TELEPHONE** 21 65 950
OPENING HOURS MON-FRI 15.00-18.30, SAT 11.00-15.00
CREDIT CARDS NONE **U-BAHNHOF** NOLLENDORFPLATZ

You may have seen it at flea markets: Used office furniture. Although old cupboards and shelves are not very beautiful to look at, there is something fascinating about old office furniture that makes it so attractive for modern living. And with its patina it not only looks better, it's usually cheaper than the metal cupboards you can buy at chic designer shops. Das alte Bureau ('the old office') stocks old shelving and storage furniture from as early as the 1920s and as far away as Sweden and America. Considering the furniture is in mint condition, the prices are excellent.

Take a trip around the world without ever leaving this store. The owner of Up-Arts, Ulrike Neuß, has traveled through Kalimantan, Papua New Guinea, Sumatra, Bhutan, Tibet, Nagaland, Rajasthan, Gujarat, Orissa, Madhya Pradesh, Pakistan and Turkmenistan to get silver jewelry, masks, amulets, baskets, sculptures and textiles for her shop. It's literally stacked to the roof. As she has collected all the pieces herself, Mrs. Neuß can tell you stories about the function, origin and meaning of the thousands of items she sells. If you are into handicrafts from Asia and Oceania, or if you're simply looking for an exotic gift item, Up-Arts is worth the trip.

Up-Arts
tribal arts

GOLTZSTRASSE 12 **TELEPHONE** 21 69 021
OPENING HOURS MON-FRI 11.00-19.00, SAT 11.00-16.00
CREDIT CARDS NONE **U-BAHNHOF** NOLLENDORFPLATZ

Almirah is more than a store; it's a gallery. The owners, Douglas Rathgeber and Willy Esser, regularly travel through Asia looking for exotic furniture. To keep the range of products in the store unique, they order small quantities or even one-off pieces. Wooden furniture and unique cupboards made from recycled antique wooden planks, doors and windows fill the store. This truly is "furniture that tells stories", as the slogan says.

Almirah
exotic furniture gallery

GOLTZSTRASSE 48 **TELEPHONE** 21 68 679
OPENING HOURS MON-FRI 12.00-19.00, SAT 11.00-16.00
CREDIT CARDS NONE **U-BAHNHOF** NOLLENDORFPLATZ

Groopie De Luxe

freaky fashion

GOLTZSTRASSE 39 **TELEPHONE** 21 72 038
OPENING HOURS MON-FRI 11.00-19.00, SAT 11.00-16.00
CREDIT CARDS VISA, AMEX, MASTERCARD **U-BAHNHOF** NOLLENDORFPLATZ

155

For a tour of Berlin's up-and-coming fashion talent, there's no better place than Groopie De Luxe. Although the name suggests rock 'n' roll, this is a store for those living 'la vida loca'. You'll find asymmetrical skirts, silver-sequined nylon jackets, customized combat gear and recycled fashion, but no big brands here. This store exclusively stocks fashion by young Berlin designers like Betty Bund, 3000 fashion and many others whose names are not known yet. It's loud fashion with a sometimes-ironic edge.

Roberta

fine fast food

GOLTZSTRASSE 34 **TELEPHONE** 21 75 39 50
OPENING HOURS MON-SAT 08.30-22.00, SUN 09.30-22.00
CREDIT CARDS NONE **PRICE** SNACK € 6 **U-BAHNHOF** NOLLENDORFPLATZ

156

Be honest. Even the best of us have a taste for fast food once in a while. When the craving hits you, it's time to visit Roberta. This is true fast food heaven with a special quality. Here you'll get freshly made burgers, pancakes and sandwiches, fries cut from real potatoes, pasta, Tramezzini and delicious salads for only € 3 to € 8. It's all fresh, delicious and served in good sized portions. Fancy a customized meal? For a 'portion Americano', add a little coleslaw, the US version of good old German 'Krautsalat'. Ketchup flows freely but Marlboro Men and Gauloises Blondes stay outside, as this snack bar is a smoke-free zone.

There are lots of cafés and bars on Goltzstrasse, but none has a breakfast as good as Savo. There's an Italian version, a Spanish one and of course the usual luxuries of a continental breakfast. The bacon is delicious and the fruits served so fresh it's as if they've just been plucked from a tree. If you'd rather have a salad than a heavy breakfast, go ahead, they are equally good. At night, this is a good spot for flirtation and cocktails. If you can't find anyone to flirt with, sit back, watch others at work and browse through the extensive choice of reading material on the windowsill.

Savo
breakfast classics

GOLTZSTRASSE 3 **TELEPHONE** 21 66 225
OPENING HOURS DAILY 09.00-02.00
CREDIT CARDS NONE **PRICE** € 6 **U-BAHNHOF** EISENACHERSTRASSE

It's rare to find a place where you can have a proper cup of tea in Germany, one of the world's leading coffee drinking nations. Luckily, there's TTT, where you can chose from more than 140 different kinds of tea from all over the world. TTT's specialty is green tea, and they really know how to brew it. If you're feeling hungry, try one of the homemade cakes or salads. And don't worry... there's no prejudice against coffee here. Caffeine addicts can still get their fix here. But smokers beware - this house of tea is smoke-free!

TeeTeaThé
house of tea

GOLTZSTRASSE 2 **TELEPHONE** 21 75 22 40
OPENING HOURS MON–FRI 09.00-24.00, SAT 10.00-24.00
CREDIT CARDS VISA, MASTERCARD **U-BAHNHOF** NOLLENDORFPLATZ

Habibi

middle eastern delights

AKAZIENSTRASSE 9 **TELEPHONE** 78 74 428
OPENING HOURS DAILY 11.00-02.00
CREDIT CARDS NONE **PRICE** € 8 **U-BAHNHOF** EISENACHERSTRASSE

159

Habibi has won several prizes for its freshly made Middle Eastern food. It's so popular amongst Berliners that there are three restaurants to choose from, this one at Akazienstrasse being the latest to open. Check out a falafel, try one of the tabouli plates for € 7 and wash it down with carrot or orange juice. To finish that off, have a strong tea or one of the deliciously sweet pastries. It's all freshly made, excellently presented, and if it weren't always so crowded, would be just perfect. But isn't the crowd a sign of quality?

Vom Winde Verweht

gone with the wind

EISENACHERSTRASSE 81 **TELEPHONE** 78 70 36 36
OPENING HOURS MON-FRI 10.00-13.00 & 14.30-18.30, SAT 10.00-14.00
CREDIT CARDS AMEX, VISA, MASTERCARD **U-BAHNHOF** EISENACHERSTRASSE

This is probably the best shop name anyone can come up with for
a place specializing in things that can be thrown up into the air. Vom
Winde verweht is a shop for kites; with prices ranging from € 5 to
€ 1500. It's also where jugglers go to buy their batons and where
serious frisbee throwers go to buy their professional air-gear. Service
is thorough here, so if your kite crashes (and it's not completely
wrecked) they'll fix it for you professionally. If your kite does happen
to run with the wind, go in and choose a new one from the wide
selection in stock. The clerks will be happy to give you advice on
how to hold on to this one!

Try a spicy fish soup or lamb liver in mint with glazed carrots, and you'll understand why Cheban has been written up, for two years in a row, in the world-renowned French restaurant guide, Gault Millau. Serving authentic Lebanese cooking, the food at Cheban is fantastic - though the service could be friendlier. If the thought of Lebanese food conjures up cheap falafel sandwiches for you, it's time to explore the complexities of the cuisine - and there's no better place than Cheban!

Cheban
lebanese food

WARTBURGSTRASSE 41 **TELEPHONE** 78 84 295
OPENING HOURS TUE-SUN 18.00-24.00
CREDIT CARDS NONE **PRICE** € 17 **U-BAHNHOF** BAYRISCHERPLATZ

For a truly Alsatian experience, try Storch. You'll sit at a long wooden table, rubbing shoulders with your fellow diners delighting at the tarte flambé, wonderful cheese board, wild boar and quails. Choose a delicate Alsatian wine or France's most popular beer, Kronenbourg. Top off your meal with an excellent brandy. Reservations are essential, as Storch is always buzzing. Vegetarians beware; Alsatian cuisine is heavy on meat, but if you ask in enough time, the multilingual crew can put something together for you.

Storch
alsatian cooking

WARTBURGSTRASSE 54 **TELEPHONE** 78 42 059
OPENING HOURS DAILY 18.00-02.00
CREDIT CARDS VISA, MASTERCARD **PRICE** € 18 **U-BAHNHOF** EISENACHERSTRASSE

Edd's
true thai treats

LÜTZOWSTRASSE 81 **TELEPHONE** 21 55 294
OPENING HOURS TUE-FRI 12.00-24.00, SAT, SUN 14.00-24.00
CREDIT CARDS NONE **PRICE** € 20 **U-BAHNHOF** KURFÜRSTENSTRASSE

163

Even many Thais consider this the best Thai restaurant outside of their homeland. Cooking is in Edd's blood. His grandmother cooked at the Thai Royal palace in Bangkok, but Edd has taken Thai cuisine to a new level. His inventions, such as his famous "hotpot", tingle the taste buds and have made this restaurant extremely popular with artists, curators, film industry moguls and the rich and famous. The Edd's experience doesn't come cheap, however, € 15 and up for a main course, and the restaurant is always busy, so make sure to reserve a table early.

Hakuin
meatless pleasures

MARTIN-LUTHERSTRASSE 1 **TELEPHONE** 21 82 027
OPENING HOURS DAILY 10.00-01.00
CREDIT CARDS NONE **PRICE** € 15 **U-BAHNHOF** SCHÖNLEINSTRASSE

Run by very friendly Zen-Buddhists, Hakuin is a definite must for vegetarians and fans of veg-cuisine. It's a smoke-free environment where you can get the best vegetarian food in town. Asian, Indian, Mediterranean; all meatless, some of it even vegan (without animal fats). Try, for example, the Kabuki, a Japanese dish with Gyozas (dough bags stuffed with vegetables), Tempeh (fermented soybeans), shiitake mushrooms, brown rice and lemon sauce for € 17. Its not only exotic tasting, it also looks fantastic, as does the whole restaurant, which resembles a Buddhist temple.

Charlottenburg

Before the fall of the Berlin Wall, Charlottenburg was the most prominent neighborhood in the city. The Kurfürstendamm is worth a visit even today, with its many offices and shops. This is where you'll find KaDeWe, Berlin's answer to Harrods or Macy's. The alleys off Kurfürstendamm are even more interesting to explore. This guide focuses on the area of Savignyplatz, Bleibtreustrasse and Kantstrasse, where some of Berlin's most exquisite shops and best restaurants are located. Charlottenburg is also where Berlin's most affluent residents live and play. You'll notice this in the dense population of luxury vehicles and the higher price tags on food and entertainment. Berlin's heart beats in other areas these days, but Charlottenburg still holds a dominant position in the city's commercial and cultural arenas.

Charlottenburg

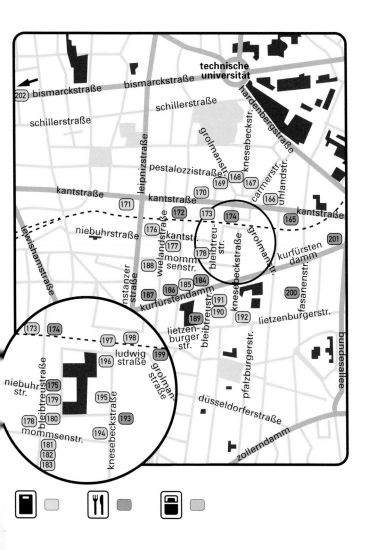

This restaurant could easily be mistaken for a contemporary art exhibit; there's so much of it hanging on the walls. Many artists who have visited Paris Bar have left works of art as payment or gifts of thanks. The lumpy street lamp in the front, for example, is by the late Martin Kippenberger, who was a regular customer. Many international celebrities have wined and dined here, and during the Berlin film festival Paris Bar is full of stars. And the food? It's French, it's expensive, and people like Robert de Niro and Milla Jovovich - who come here when they're in Berlin - love it.

Paris Bar
legendary restaurant

KANTSTRASSE 152 **TELEPHONE** 31 38 052
OPENING HOURS DAILY 12.00-02.00
CREDIT CARDS AMEX, VISA **PRICE** € 25 **U-BAHNHOF** UHLANDSTRASSE

165

If you're not in the mood to stroll all around Charlottenburg popping into interior design stores, then head for Stilwerk. Spread over five floors, there are 52 stores here offering everything a style-conscious buyer can think of. There are kitchen and bathroom stores; a design- and photo-gallery; a boutique for colored fabrics; stores for ceramics, glass, lighting, wood and plastics, etc., etc. It would be impossible to mention everything! The place lacks atmosphere, but if you like shopping malls and all forms of design, Stilwerk is definitely worth a look.

Stilwerk
temple of style

KANTSTRASSE CORNER UHLANDSTRASSE **TELEPHONE** 31 51 50
OPENING HOURS MON-FRI 10.00-20.00, SAT 10.00-16.00
CREDIT CARDS VISA, AMEX, MASTERCARD **S-BAHNHOF** SAVIGNYPLATZ

Riccardo Cortillone

shoes, italian style

SAVIGNYPLATZ 4 **TELEPHONE** 31 29 701
OPENING HOURS MON–FRI 10.00-20.00, SAT 10.00-16.00
CREDIT CARDS VISA, AMEX, MASTERCARD **S-BAHNHOF** SAVIGNYPLATZ

Rock singer Mink De Ville once sang: "There's something about me that women all love: it's my Italian shoes". The tiger-striped shoes worn on the cover of that single aren't available here, but tons of other Italian shoes are. New ones arrive every other week; always the latest in Italian shoe fashions, for both men and women. Just across the street, is an affiliated store where you'll find 'bargains'; i.e. shoes from last season or ones used for display. Surely, they're "always in style", just as Mink De Ville sang.

Zeppelin
back to basics

 SAVIGNYPLATZ 4 **TELEPHONE** 017 23 11 14 48
OPENING HOURS MON-FRI 10.00-20.00, SAT 10.00-16.00
CREDIT CARDS VISA, AMEX, MASTERCARD **S-BAHNHOF** SAVIGNYPLATZ

Zeppelin is the perfect place to pick up basic, yet
stylish, fashions. With three branches in Berlin, it's a
very popular alternative to the similarly styled American
chain stores found here. The store carries both men's
and women's fashion - quite chic, but not extravagant.
Prices are moderate too, making this a great place to
go for clothes that make you look good without going
overboard, both in style and in price.

Rio's jewelry makes regular appearances in fashion magazines, films, and advertising and at grand, lavish receptions. This is jewelry for big occasions, both day and night. The shop's owner, Barbara Kranz, has been in business for 17 years and has certainly got what it takes when it comes to producing and selling elegant jewelry. There are over 1000 different choices - from rings to beads and necklaces - in different shapes, colors and materials. The store has its own collections made twice yearly. Be sure to bring wads of cash... credit cards are not accepted!

Rio
grand jewelry

BLEIBTREUSTRASSE 52 **TELEPHONE** 31 33 152
OPENING HOURS MON-WED, FRI 11.00-18.30, THU 11.00-19.00, SAT 11.00-16.00
CREDIT CARDS NONE **S-BAHNHOF** SAVIGNYPLATZ

169

Avid film collectors know how hard it is to find a store that carries as wide a selection as this. M sucht nach Film offers a huge range of original, un-subtitled versions of films on video. Also available is an invaluable, free research service for those hard-to-get films. The shelves here are filled with Hollywood classics, as well as European and Asian movies, films for special interests, nature and travel-videos, kid's movies and gay & lesbian cinema. DVDs and Laserdiscs are available too. Before you go, check out the store's website, and search for yourself.

M Sucht Nach Film

experts for films and videos

KANTSTRASSE 28 **TELEPHONE** 26 24 321 WWW.MSUCHTNACHFILM.DE
OPENING HOURS MON-FRI 11 00-19.00, SAT 11.00-16.00
CREDIT CARDS VISA, AMEX, MASTERCARD **S-BAHNHOF** SAVIGNYPLATZ

Iran Shop

specialities from iran

KANTSTRASSE 124 **TELEPHONE** 31 25 568
OPENING HOURS MON–FRI 09.30-18.30, SAT 09.30-14.00
CREDIT CARDS NONE **S-BAHNHOF** SAVIGNYPLATZ

For Iranians, this store is like a piece of home. For others, it's a wonderful opportunity to experience a taste of Iranian culture. In addition to edible delicacies such as nuts, dried fruits, Iranian spices, sweets and soft drinks, there is a huge selection of tapes and CDs of traditional music, plus books and videos for rent and sale. The friendly man behind the counter tell us that people come from all over to buy the specialties at his store... Apparently it's the only Iranian store in Berlin.

Samurai

great japanese cooking

WILMERSDORFERSTRASSE 22 **TELEPHONE** 34 14 184
OPENING HOURS DAILY 12.00-15.00
CREDIT CARDS NONE **PRICE** PLATE OF SUSHI € 7 **U-BAHNHOF** BISMARCKSTRASSE

The interior of this restaurant, with its low tables, rice-paper walls and Japanese lamps, is so authentic that it's easy to imagine yourself in a noodle house in Japan. The food is excellent, and prices are moderate. A plate of sushi (12 pieces) is available for € 6; add a Sapporo and miso soup to start and you still barely break the € 10 barrier. The fact that Japanese tourists and business people come here for lunch is a ringing endorsement in itself!

There are a lot of hot young French designers who are not as well known as the haute couture names, but who make 'pret-a-porter' fashion with similar elegance. L'Orange is a great place to find the work of this new breed. The store sells women's fashions from la Grande Nation - everything except shoes. The interior is bright and colorful, and French pop music gets you in the French mode. Francophiles can speak French with the employees, but no French kissing!

L'Orange
french and funky

BLEIBTREUSTRASSE 5A **TELEPHONE** 31 50 48 83
OPENING HOURS MON-FRI 10.00-20.00, SAT 10.00-16.00
CREDIT CARDS VISA, AMEX, MASTERCARD **S-BAHNHOF** SAVIGNYPLATZ

Zwölf Apostel is considered one of the best Italian restaurants in Berlin, so popular that there are two other branches in other parts of the city. The marble floor and paintings on the ceiling give it the proper Italian ambience, with dim lighting and a live pianist at night. In addition to the lovely interior, the stone-oven pizzas are baked 24 hours a day, and are what Zwölf Apostel is famous for. Some say they are the best in town. If you have a big appetite, come for the all-you-can-eat Pizza Party on Mondays, but make sure you reserve a table ahead of time; it's a very popular event amongst locals.

Zwölf Apostel

stone oven pizzas

BLEIBTREUSTRASSE 49 **TELEPHONE** 31 21 433
OPENING HOURS DAILY 24 HOURS
CREDIT CARDS NONE **PRICE** € 10 **S-BAHNNHOF** SAVIGNYPLATZ

Ali Baba

hot pizza

BLEIBTREUSTRASSE 45 **TELEPHONE** 88 11 350
OPENING HOURS DAILY 11.00-03.00
CREDIT CARDS AMEX, VISA, MASTERCARD **PRICE** PIZZA € 6 **S-BAHNHOF** SAVIGNYPLATZ

Ali Baba is a Charlottenburg classic, and has been around for years. A fresh pizza is made here every three minutes, and a slice with green peppers is just € 1. The place is run by Arabs who have given it an authentic feel by decorating it with the Italian red, white and green throughout. The food is good and wine is OK; this is not a serious option for a romantic evening, but it's just right for a quick snack.

Emma & Co

fashion for infants

NIEBUHRSTRASSE 1 **TELEPHONE** 88 27 373
OPENING HOURS MON-WED 11.00-18.30, THU, FRI 11.00-19.30, SAT 11.00-16.00
CREDIT CARDS VISA, AMEX, MASTERCARD **S-BAHNHOF** SAVIGNYPLATZ

You have to walk through Bramigk & Breer, an interior design store, to get to Emma & Co. If you can get past all the items for your home in the first store, you'll find yourself surrounded by basic, but unique clothes for kids. These are individualistic togs, without the hype of big-brand clothing. The small, personal and neat store offers everything from shoes to accessories, playthings and girls' and boys' clothing from Italy and France. The split-store approach is quite clever; one concept ideal for the whole family.

This elegant boutique is for women who like to wear luxurious outfits, without spending a fortune. Madonna carries second hand designer clothes, priced at about half the original cost. Last summer's slipdress from Dolce & Gabbana is available for € 150. Almost brand-new Prada shoes go for € 140. Everything is in mint condition; the only thing that reminds you it's used is the incredibly low prices. Madonna also stocks brand-new bags by names such as Dior or Fendi that also go for good prices. This is definitely the place for material girls.

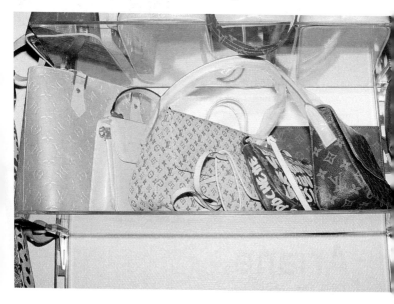

Madonna
material girl

MOMMSENSTRASSE 57 **TELEPHONE** 31 44 37 82
OPENING HOURS MON–FRI 11.00-19.00, SAT 11.00-15.00
CREDIT CARDS VISA **S-BAHNHOF** SAVIGNYPLATZ

Have you ever eyed a tweed Chanel jacket with golden buttons, then had a heart attack when you looked at the price tag? Come to Ariane, where you'll be able to find one at about a third of the regular price; the fact that it was once worn by a successful lawyer, doctor or actress might just make it feel that much more comfortable. In addition to Chanel, dresses, shirts and other clothes by names like Versus, Prada and D&G are available, as are a huge selection of shoes, accessories, sunglasses and jewelry.

Ariane
used designer gear

MOMMSENSTRASSE 4 **TELEPHONE** NO
OPENING HOURS MON–FRI 11.00-18.30, SAT 10.00-15.00
CREDIT CARDS VISA, MASTERCARD **S-BAHNHOF** SAVIGNYPLATZ

Kaufhaus Schrill

kitsch shopping

BLEIBTREUSTRASSE 46 **TELEPHONE** 88 24 048
OPENING HOURS MON-FRI 12.00-19.00, SAT 11.00-16.00
CREDIT CARDS VISA, AMEX, MASTERCARD **S-BAHNHOF** SAVIGNYPLATZ

In German, "schrill" is a word typi-
cally used in the 80s to describe
freaky and weird things and
situations. Thus, it's the perfect
name for this boutique, which
specializes in offbeat items. Take,
for example, the cufflinks that
say: "I'm the boss", or: "I'm
never wrong", or ties with the
members of Kiss emblazoned on
them. Perhaps you'll be entran-
ced instead by the colorful feather
boas, the tons of wonderful fake
jewelry, or the faux gold and
silver chains, the wigs, the
hats or one of the other many
funny and useless items.
Kitsch lovers should not
miss this shop.

Paint Your Style
ideas on ceramics

 BLEIBTREUSTRASSE 46 **TELEPHONE** 88 55 22 23 WWW.PAINTYOURSTYLE.DE
OPENING HOURS MON-SUN 11.00-22.00
CREDIT CARDS VISA, AMEX, MASTERCARD **S-BAHNHOF** SAVIGNYPLATZ

The "paint your own pottery" concept that swept across
North America has now reached the shores of Europe.
At Paint your style, you can sit down in bright and friendly
surroundings, and paint on raw china in the shape of
plates, vases or cups. At € 7 for the raw material plus
€ 8 for each hour you paint, it's a nice way to while away
an afternoon. And, three days later, you'll end up with a
totally personalized souvenir. It may not be the cheapest
coffee mug you could buy, but what could be more
unique than something you painted yourself?

Art & Industry is a store for real furniture lovers. From art deco to 1970s modern, the store showcases select objects, single pieces and groups of furniture from 20th century Germany, Italy, Scandinavia and the US. Whether it's a chair by Marcel Breuer or a table by Mies van der Rohe, Art & Industry has it all, as well as porcelain, ceramics and vintage electrical devices. On Tuesday afternoons, check out their larger storeroom at Wilmersdorferstrasse 39, where an even greater assortment is displayed. A trip to Art & Industry is like a visit to an interior design museum. The only difference is that here, everything is for sale.

Art & Industry

classic furniture

BLEIBTREUSTRASSE 40 **TELEPHONE** 88 34 936 WWW.ARTINDUSTRY.DE
OPENING HOURS MON-FRI 14.00-18.30, SAT 11.00-16.00
CREDIT CARDS VISA, AMEX, MASTERCARD **S-BAHNHOF** SAVIGNYPLATZ

Women in fancy Charlottenburg always seem to dress up more than in other parts of the city. All this glamour has got to end up somewhere, and Chiara is the first choice for the ladies of the area, where almost everything carries a designer's name. This is the place to find 1970s Chanel shoes, vintage YSL or, if you're lucky, an original Prada bag from the early 1980s. Take your time looking around; you're bound to come across a stunning item from fashion's recent past that you won't find anywhere else.

Chiara-Seconda Mano
first & second hand glam

BLEIBTREUSTRASSE 39 **TELEPHONE** 88 68 06 71
OPENING HOURS MON-FRI 11.00-19.00, SAT 11.00-16.00
CREDIT CARDS VISA, AMEX, MASTERCARD **S-BAHNHOF** SAVIGNYPLATZ

DK Cosmetics

top of the line cosmetics

KURFÜRSTENDAMM 56 **TELEPHONE** 32 79 01 23 WWW.DKCOSMETICS.DE
OPENING HOURS MON-FRI 10.00-19.00, SAT 10.00-16.00
CREDIT CARDS VISA, AMEX, MASTERCARD **U-BAHNHOF** UHLANDSTRASSE

I don't care how shallow it sounds: expensive cosmetics, whether for hair or body, make you feel good. How else can you look fresh in the morning after partying hard all night? DK cosmetics is the best place to find the right potions to make you look like a million bucks, even if you missed out on some beauty sleep. They carry all the top cosmetic brands, and some that are hard to get elsewhere in Europe. It may cost a lot, but can you really put a price on looking good?

Soup Kultur

berlin's no.1 soup bar

KURFÜRSTENDAMM 224 **TELEPHONE** 74 30 82 95 WWW.SOUPKULTUR.DE
OPENING HOURS MON–FRI 12.00–20.00, SAT 12.00–16.00
CREDIT CARDS NONE **PRICE** SOUP € 5 **U-BAHNHOF** KURFÜRSTENDAMM

Soup is hot, and we don't just mean literally. It is a popular food choice in London, New York and even in Berlin. And why not? Soup is quick, nutritious and gives you warmth and energy. One of the world's oldest and simplest dishes, it is made in endless variations and is found in every cuisine. Soup Kultur has some fantastic variations, all freshly made, with spice or without, with meat or without, for € 4 to € 6. The menu is always changing, and if you are in a hurry, you can get take out. Check out the website for current menu offerings and some recipes.

King's Teagarden has a fantastic assortment of tea and accessories for preparing and consuming the leaf. There are hundreds of different kinds of teas here, from variants of Darjeeling to teas for stimulating your love life. You'll find the most popular teas as well as more exotic and intriguing varieties. If you want to try before you buy, visit the tasting room, where you can try sips of the different teas from small cups. Just your cup of tea...

King's Teagarden

tea for two, or more

KURFÜRSTENDAMM 217 **TELEPHONE** 88 37 059 WWW.KINGSTEAGARDEN.DE
OPENING HOURS MON–FRI 10.00-20.00, SAT 10.00-16.00
CREDIT CARDS VISA, AMEX **U-BAHNHOF** KURFÜRSTENSTRASSE

Caras

gourmet coffee

WIELANDSTRASSE 11 **TELEPHONE** 85 96 59 65
OPENING HOURS MON-FRI 08.00-21.30, SAT 09.00-21.30, SUN 10.00-20.00
CREDIT CARDS NONE **PRICE** SNACK € 2.50 **U-BAHNHOF** UHLANDSTRASSE

The wave of American-style coffeehouse chains that has swept through Europe recently has luckily not yet reached Berlin. Maybe that's because the city already has so many good cafés. Caras is a great example. It offers practically the same range of coffees you'd find in an average Starbucks, but it's self-service and the drinks and sandwiches taste fresher and are not as expensive. Service is very quick and if the weather is good, you can sit outside and watch passers-by on Kudamm.

Tons of Italian delicacies are offered up at I briganti, from fresh anti-pasti selections to pasta, sauces and cheeses. To complement the food, a great variety of Italian wines are also available. At lunchtime, try something warm; a different dish is served every day. This is a good option for vegetarians too, with two meat-less specials on the menu daily.

I Briganti
mio amore

WIELANDSTRASSE 15 **TELEPHONE** 32 35 362
OPENING HOURS MON-FRI 10.00-20.00, SAT 10.00-16.00
CREDIT CARDS NONE **PRICE** € 8 **S-BAHNHOF** SAVIGNYPLATZ

Sehmänner

making eyes

BLEIBTREUSTRASSE 27 **TELEPHONE** 88 55 24 24
OPENING HOURS MON–FRI 10.00-20.00, SAT 10.00-16.00
CREDIT CARDS VISA, AMEX, MASTERCARD **S-BAHNHOF** SAVIGNYPLATZ

There might not be a better way to change your look than to get new glasses. Head to Sehmänner (which means 'men who see'), for a wide collection of frames. If you don't like what you see, ask for the individually manufactured glasses made from natural horn. They are not cheap but they're fabulous and absolutely unique. For more conventional tastes, many designer brands are also in stock.

Ein & Dreißig is just off Kurfürstendamm, so if you're a bit hungry after a full day of shopping, take a load off at this small snack bar. Named after its street number (31), guests at nearby Hotel Bleibtreu have their breakfast here, but it's also open to the public. The menu includes fresh sandwiches, bagels and small cakes, as well as freshly squeezed juices and a variety of coffees. During lunch hour, full meals are served, priced from € 8 to € 12, with a menu that changes daily. All the food is light, with a Californian/Mediterranean feeling. If you are very hungry, visit the restaurant in the back, where various courses are offered.

Ein & Dreißig
snack bar

BLEIBTREUSTRASSE 31 **TELEPHONE** 88 47 46 03
OPENING HOURS MON-SAT 08.00-22.00, SUN 09.00-18.00
CREDIT CARDS VISA, AMEX, MASTERCARD **PRICE** € 10 **U-BAHNHOF** UHLANDSTRASSE

For more than a decade, Bleibgrün has been the purveyor of exclusive shoes and fashion. The store is not about big brand hype, but about personal style. Consequently, it's philosophy is to stock designer wear with an individual edge. Some of the designs are a little elaborate, but storeowner Karuma Ouali keeps an eye out for the right balance. You might find a few big names, but most of the clothes and shoes here are by up-and-coming talent or designers who have not yet made a name. Independent, self-assured women who know what they like, will definitely like Bleibgrün.

Bleibgrün
exclusive shoes and fashion

190

BLEIBTREUSTRASSE 29 & 30 **TELEPHONE** 88 21 689
OPENING HOURS MON-FRI 10.30-20.00, SAT 10.30-16.00
CREDIT CARDS VISA, AMEX, MASTERCARD **S-BAHNHOF** SAVIGNYPLATZ

Hartog
interior accessories

KNESEBECKSTRASSE 68 **TELEPHONE** 88 37 929
OPENING HOURS MON-FRI 10.00-20.00, SAT 10.00-16.00
CREDIT CARDS VISA, AMEX, MASTERCARD **S-BAHNHOF** SAVIGNYPLATZ

The range of products here is so vast that it's quite difficult to identify the store's focus. The best term is probably 'interior accessories': that is, everything and anything you need to furnish your home or kitchen. Most of the products come from Scandinavia and Italy, although some are German. To be sure, everything is top quality. If your own home is already well equipped, you'll definitely be able to find some nice presents for friends and family. Hartog is not super-trendy; rather, it caters to those with their feet firmly on the ground.

Rosewater's
beauty health and care

KNESEBECKSTRASSE 5 **TELEPHONE** 31 50 30 22
OPENING HOURS MON–FRI 10.00-19.30, SAT 10.00-16.00
CREDIT CARDS NONE **S-BAHNHOF** SAVIGNYPLATZ

The smells from Rosewater's reach you from hundreds of feet away.
The products sold here have intense aromas, and when they merge
together the whole street smells of flowers. When the store opened
in 1991, it sold only English beauty items, but now it has become
'Europeanized,' with health and beauty care products from all over the
continent. Rosewater's stocks lotions, bath oils, body care products,
natural cosmetics, incense sticks and essential oils. The shop's employees give good advice on choosing the perfect item for therapy
or beauty. Take a deep breath and enjoy.

If you agree with the title of that Smiths album from the 1980s ("Meat is murder"), then Einhorn is the ideal snack bar for you. It's full of natural, ecological food, and at lunchtime a giant variety of delicious and fresh salads, vegetable platters, pastas and cheese plates are available from € 6 to € 10. Eco-wines and fruit drinks are available too, and there's almost nothing a connoisseur of good, healthy food will miss in this place. Einhorn also offers a catering service, with an even broader range of fine food.

Einhorn
meatless treats

MOMMSENSTRASSE 2 **TELEPHONE** 21 12 504
OPENING HOURS MON-FRI 09.00-18.30
CREDIT CARDS NONE **PRICE** € 8 **S-BAHNHOF** SAVIGNYPLATZ

For passionate cooks, Der Küchenladen is absolute heaven. Every imaginable kitchen device can be found here. You dream it and they stock it: pans for steaming fish or grilling vegetables, lobster-tongs, salt and pepper grinders, pots, dishes, cutlery or even a hi-tech corkscrew for € 199. Yes, prices at Der Küchenladen are sometimes a bit absurd, but you can be assured that anything you buy will always be of the utmost quality stainless steel, wood or porcelain. If you are a serious cook or want to become one, definitely pay a visit to this store.

Der Küchenladen
cook's shop

KNESEBECKSTRASSE 26-27 **TELEPHONE** 88 55 47 26
OPENING HOURS MON-FRI 10.00-19.00, SAT 10.00-16.00
CREDIT CARDS VISA, AMEX, MASTERCARD **S-BAHNHOF** SAVIGNYPLATZ

Marga Schöller Bücherstube

institution for books

KNESEBECKSTRASSE 33 **TELEPHONE** 88 11 112
OPENING HOURS MON–WED 09.30-19.00, THU, FRI 09.30-20.00, SAT 09.30-16.00
CREDIT CARDS VISA, AMEX, MASTERCARD **S-BAHNHOF** SAVIGNYPLATZ

This bookstore has been around for more than 70 years and is one of the best-known stores in all of Berlin. Although it's right around the corner from Bücherbogen, the two don't step on each other's toes much as their concepts are completely different. Marga Schoeller stocks German literature but is mostly known for its huge variety of English books. The range covers many fields, such as travel, film, dance, theatre, music and the humanities. Bookworms be warned; you'll probably be here for hours!

Bücherbogen

international bookshop

196

SAVIGNYPLATZ 593 **TELEPHONE** 31 32 515
OPENING HOURS MON-FRI 10.00-20.00, SAT 10.00-16.00
CREDIT CARDS VISA, AMEX, MASTERCARD **S-BAHNHOF** SAVIGNYPLATZ

For Berliners, Bücherbogen is an institution...
Anyone looking for books on art, architecture,
design, fashion, theory or new media heads
here first. The store is huge and it's possible
to browse through the shelves for hours. There
are so many books, it's hard not to want to
pick them all up! If you are looking for something special, the expert employees can
surely help, and a special order service is
available. Around the corner from the main
store, at Knesebeckstrasse 27, is an outlet
where they sell discontinued and bargain
books. Be sure to check them both out.

Arno, founded in 1927, is a tradition in Berlin and has stocked modernist lamps from its beginning. The selection comes from Italy, Spain, Switzerland and Scandinavia, and ranges from minimalist ceiling lights to more decorative table lamps and chandeliers. Around the corner at Otto-Ludwigstrasse 27, is a small outlet where you'll find reduced showroom items as well as some bargains. A trip here could be quite enlightening!

Arno
light of my life

SAVIGNYPLATZ 590 **TELEPHONE** 31 59 490
OPENING HOURS MON-FRI 10.00-20.00, SAT 10.00-16.00
CREDIT CARDS VISA, AMEX, MASTERCARD **S-BAHNHOF** SAVIGNYPLATZ

197

Does your old sofa need a new cover? Got some cushions lying around that need a new look? Check out Seidlein & Seidlein, which has a huge range of beautiful fabrics to suit every whim. Styles range from 'country home' to 'urban cool', from basic to extravagant. The store also carries stylish vases, pots, and furniture. If you have any questions or need advice, the staff at Seidlein & Seidlein is very competent and will be happy to guide you.

Seidlein & Seidlein
fabrics, furniture and fun

GROHLMANNSTRASSE 37 **TELEPHONE** 31 24 480
OPENING HOURS MON–FRI 11.00-20.00, SAT 10.00-16.00
CREDIT CARDS VISA, AMEX, MASTERCARD **S-BAHNHOF** SAVIGNYPLATZ

Café Wintergarten

literary break

FASANENSTRASSE 23 **TELEPHONE** 88 25 414
OPENING HOURS DAILY 09.30-01.00
CREDIT CARDS VISA, AMEX, MASTERCARD **PRICE** € 6 **U-BAHNHOF** KURFÜRSTENDAMM

When you've strolled all over Ku'Damm and your feet need a little time to relax, the Café Wintergarten is the perfect place to take a rest. In summer, sit in the wonderful garden, or sit cozily inside in the winter. The café is known for its great cakes, and the salads and small dishes are also worth a try. Because of its location, on the ground floor of the Charlottenburg literature house, you'll see people reading or philosophizing while enjoying a cup of tea or coffee. Join in, or flip through one of the many newspapers offered to customers.

Salomon Bagels

the roll with a hole

JOACHIMSTALERSTRASSE 13 **TELEPHONE** 88 18 196
OPENING HOURS SUN-THU 08.00-22.00, FRI 08.00-01.00, SAT 08.00-02.00
CREDIT CARDS NONE **PRICE** BAGEL € 6 **U-BAHNHOF** KURFÜRSTENDAMM

For Andreas Pfeiffer, the owner of Salomon Bagels, the well-known Jewish specialty is more than a snack. It's a spiritual object, a metaphor for holiness, and a symbol for water and fire. "Wisdom to eat," he says. Whatever it means to you, these bagels are fresh and delicious. Pick up some wine or coffee and enjoy.

For years, Engelbecken has been one of the best restaurants in Kreuzberg. Now that it's located in Charlottenburg, there are more reasons to pay the restaurant a visit. The Bavarian/Austrian cuisine is as excellent as ever and the friendly crew remains almost the same. Try some of the original Bavarian "Weiswürstl" or the delicious "Rehgulasch". The list of beers on the menu is equally exquisite; they even serve the excellent Hefeweizen from the small brewery, Unertl. The restaurant is a little off the beaten track, but if you want to have the best in original German and Austrian food, it's worth a visit.

Engelbecken
bavarian and austrian specialities

WITZLEBENSTRASSE 31 **TELEPHONE** 61 52 810
OPENING HOURS MON–SAT 16.00-01.00, SUN 12.00-01.00
CREDIT CARDS VISA, MASTERCARD **PRICE** € 12 **U-BAHNHOF** SOPHIE-CHARLOTTEPLATZ

Klingenberg specialises in renting office and design furniture to large companies. If you've ever dreamed of owning an original Knoll chair or a sofa by Mies van der Rohe, then this might be the perfect store for you. When the furniture is returned from the renter, it's available for sale, and it's possible to pick up an original item for the price of a copy. Not everything is second hand either; there is also a good selection of new items at low prices. Design junkies should get check out their website online.

Klingenberg
top design for less

FRANKLINSTRASSE 12A **TELEPHONE** 39 40 680 WWW.KLINGENBERG.ORG
OPENING HOURS MON–WED 10.00–19.00, SAT 10.00–16.00
CREDIT CARDS VISA, MASTERCARD **U-BAHNHOF** ERNST-REUTER-PLATZ

Info & Index

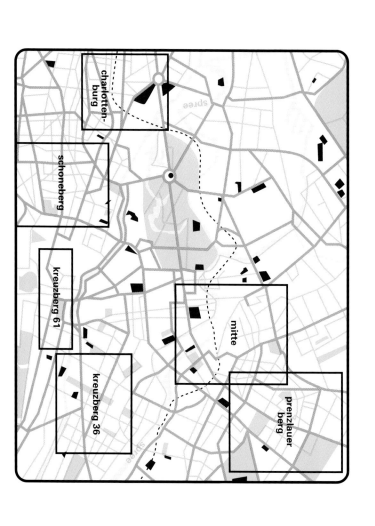

charlotten-
burg

schoneberg

kreuzberg 61

kreuzberg 36

spree

mitte

prenzlauer
berg

spree

transport

Berlin has a good underground system, which will easily take you to and from any of the areas, described in this guide. But unlike in other cities the difference between tram and tube stations isn't very obvious. As you can see on the map there is a U-bahn and a S-bahn. The first runs underground and the second over ground and you can switch from one to the other on the same ticket. Don't give up after your first try gets you lost, the system really does work.

If you're planning on using the subway a lot, it's worth informing about travel cards for one or more days, they're definitely cheaper but you have to keep your eye on the zones.

If you prefer to stay above ground, bus number 100 is your best bet. This double deck bus will lead you past Unter den Linden, Branden- burgertor, Reichstag, Schloss Bellevue, Siegessaule, Alexanderplatz and Bahnhof Zoo and you can get on and off wherever you like. Buy a one way ticket: 'Einzelfahrkart' or even better a day ticket: 'Tageskarte' at the station. The tour begins at the Zoo and it ends in Prenszlauer Berg where this guide can lead you by foot through the nicest shopping areas and take you to the best restaurants before leading you to your next wonderful destination.

markets

If you love to stroll around a market place, hunting for bargains then Berlin has loads of possibilities. We've made a selection of our favorite addresses.

TIERGARTEN
for books, art, clothing and antiques
strasse des 17 juni
s-bahnhof tiergarten
sat & sun 10.00-17.00

MITTE
for household goods, clothing, books and music
arkonaplatz
u-bahnhof bernauerstrasse
sun 10.00-16.00

MITTE
art and nostalgic markets
am kupfergraben, museuminsel
u-bahnhof friedrichstrasse
sat & sun 11.00-17.00

SCHÖNEBERG

for fruit and vegetables, bread, eco-products, clothing and jewelry

winterfeldplatz

u-bahnhof nollendorfplatz

wed & sat morning

KREUZBERG / NEUKÖLN

turkish market for fruit and vegetables, nuts and fabrics

maybachufer, schönleinstrasse

tue & fri 12.00-18.00

TREPTOW

indoor flea market

puschkinallee

u-bahnhof schlesischestor

sat & sun 10.00-18.00

sight seeing

There are many great things to do in Berlin besides shopping, eating and clubbing. It's almost impossible to sum them all up for you but here's a list of things to do and see that are definitely worth while.

ZOO
zoologischer garten,
hardenbergerplatz 8, tiergarten
U-bahnhof zoologischer garten

PERFECT VIEW
a panoramic view from the 24th floor of the new daimler chrysler building
alte potsdamerstrasse, mitte
u-bahnhof potsdamerplatz

CINEMA
3D-films in the Imax Marlene cinema
dietrichplatz 4, mitte
U-bahnhof potsdamerplatz

museums

PERGAMOM
old classics
bodestrasse, mitte
u-bahnhof friedrichstrasse

closed on mondays

CHECKPOINT CHARLIE

all the info on the rise and fall of the berlin wall

friedrichstrasse, kreuzberg

u-bahnhof kochstrasse

MARTIN GROPIUSBAU

various contemporary exhibitions

stresemannstrasse 110, kreuzberg

s-bahnhof anhalterbahnhof

closed on mondays

GEMÄLDEGALERIE AM KULTURFORUM

old masters and classic modernists

matthäikirchplatz 8, tiergarten

u-bahnhof potsdamerplatz

closed on mondays

NEUE NATIONALGALERIE

modern art gallery

potsdamerstrasse 50, tiergarten

u-bahnhof potsdamerplatz

closed on mondays

LIBESKINDBAU / JÜDISCHES MUSEUM

exhibitions on jewish life

lindenstrasse 9-14, kreuzberg

u-bahnhof kochstrasse

HAMBURGER BAHNHOF

modern art in former station

invalidenstrasse 50-51, mitte

s-bahnhof lehrter stadtbahnhof closed on mondays

lounge- & cocktailbars

It's cool to lounge around, so Berlin has many places where you can "hang out" and enjoy a soothing cocktail. These are the best ones.

COOKIES COCKTAIL BAR
gipsstrasse 7
mitte

ASTRO-BAR
simon-dachstrasse 40
friedrichshain

LORE
neue schönhauserstrasse 20
mitte

MAS Y MAS
hohenstauffenstrasse 69
schöneberg

KAFFEE BURGER
torstrasse 68
mitte

TROMPETE
lützowplatz
schöneberg

808 LOUNGE
oranienburgerstrasse 42-43
mitte

AKBA LOUNGE
sredzkistrasse 64
prenzlauer berg

SEVEN LOUNGE
ackerstrasse 20
mitte

NN-BAR
hauptstrasse 159
schöneberg

NEWTON BAR
charlottenstrasse 57
mitte

clubs

boogie on down that's what Berlin's all about and here's where you can do it best.

90 GRAD hip-hop & house
dennewitzstrasse 37
schöneberg

CASINO house & techno
saarbruckerstrasse corner
prenzlauer allee
prenzlauer berg

PFEFFERBANK dance & house
schönhauser allee 176
prenzlauer berg

BASTARD@PRATER
electro, berlin underground rock
kastanienallee 7-9
prenzlauer berg

ROTER SALON VOLKSBÜHNE
anything goes, salsa too
rosa-luxembourgplatz
mitte

ICON hip-hop, dub & drum 'n bass
cantinastrasse 15
prenzlauer berg

TRESOR techno
leipzigerstrasse 126a
mitte

SOPHIENCLUB disco, soul & 80s
sophienstrasse 6
mitte

SAGE CLUB soul, funk & house
köpernickerstrasse 78
mitte

PRIVAT KLUB live music
pücklerstrasse 34
kreuzberg

WMF drum 'n bass & (disco)house
ziegelstrasse
mitte

COOKIE'S tuesday house and techno,
thursday freestyle
charlottenstrasse 44
mitte

websites

Everything and anything you need to know about Berlin is available on the internet. If you want to make reservations in any form or if you need any information, these websites will come in handy.

WWW.BERLIN.DE general information

WWW.MEINBERLIN.DE general information

WWW.BERLINONLINE.DE general information

WWW.HOTELSTRAVEL.COM hotel reservations

WWW.ASE.NET hotel reservations

WWW.ZITTY.DE what to do in berlin, also available as a magazine as well as on the internet

category index

213

alphabetical index

also available

barcelona 90 5767 086 0

new york 90 5767 089 5

paris 90 5767 090 9

london 90 5767 088 7

amsterdam 90 5767 085 2

notes

notes

© mo' media, breda, september 2002

mo' media, attn berlin shop · eat · sleep,
postbus 7028, 4800 ga, breda, the netherlands,
e-mail info@momedia.nl